Christ our Healer

Peter Smythe

To Aisha and Alex,
my sister and my brother in Christ

First Printing 2012
ISBN: 978-0-9830033-2-8
Copyright © Peter Smythe

Table of Contents

The Divine Word...1

Origins of Sickness and Disease.......................................5
  The Initial Creation...5
  Disease: The Sin Connection..7
  Sin as a Causal Link to Disease..8
  Healing of the Blind Boy..8
  Bent-Over Woman...9

God's Method of Healing is Spiritual............................13
  Timothy's Wine..14
  Hezekiah's Poultice..15
  James's Anointing Oil...15

The Old Testament...19
  The Old Covenant...19
  Promise for the Promised Land...20
  Types and Shadows of Christ's Work................................21
    Aaron's Stay of the Plague..22
    The Passover Lamb..23
    The Bronze Snake..24
    The Healing of the Leper...25

Distributions 27
   Elijah and the Widow in Zarephath............................27
   Elisha and the Shunammite's Son..............................28
   The Gospels and the New Testament 30
   The Healing Anointing Fluxes.....................................30
   Charismata – Gifts of the Spirit..................................31
      Naaman's Leprosy...32
      The Blind Man and the Pool of Siloam.............34

Jesus' Spiritual Distribution...37
   How God Anointed Jesus...37
      Case Study: The Lunatic Boy...............................40
      Case Study: The Blind and Mute Man................41
   Degrees of Sickness and Oppression...........................41
   Jesus' Attitude Toward Sickness..................................42
   Two Problematic Translations 44
      The Blind Man...44
      Lazarus..46

Aspects of the Power...49
   Still the Need for Faith...49
   Tangible and Residual Power.......................................51
   Transmittable...52
   The Power Extended..53
   Gateway to the Gifts of the Spirit 55

He Bore Our Diseases 57
   Familiar with Sickness...59
   Borne and Carried..61
   The Day of Atonement 63
   The Believer's Grounds for Healing.....................67

The Apostles 69
   Matthew – He Bore Our Sicknesses......................69
      Just a Messianic Claim?................................71
      That It Might Be Fulfilled 73
   Peter – You Were Healed......................................75
   Paul – He Became a Curse 83

Seated with Christ..85
   Christ is Exalted..85
   Exalted with Him 87
   The Believer is to Glorify God in Body.................88
   Spiritual Quickening...88

The Church's Commission to Heal.........................91
   The Greater Works 91
   The Church Continues Jesus' Ministry................93
   The Healing Anointing Continues........................95

The Need for Faith...97
   The Mix of Faith 97
   The Eye of Faith..99
   Healing is an Accomplished Fact........................102

The Faith That Takes..105

Steps to Appropriate Healing...106

    Receive it....106

    Pray it...106

    Possess it....107

    See it. 107

Questions About Healing..109

Scriptures..119

    Old Testament...121

    New Testament..133

1

The Divine Word

Of the making of books, there is no end (Eccl 12:12).
Since the day God expelled Adam from Eden, man
hasn't stopped filling up the world with philosophies,
religions, and beliefs—all of which the Word calls
hollow. Devoid of any divine spark or voice, they're
earthly, sensual, and devilish. On his own, man hasn't
constructed a roadway to salvation. All he has done—all
he can do—is prove to himself, a million times over, just
how undone he is when he's left to his own devices.

The Word stands alone in the world as the only work
that holds the wisdom that has descended from above. It
is the only work that is God-breathed. And it's the only
work that demonstrates the contours between spirit and
soul, this world and its supernatural underpinnings. By
its own terms, it tells us just who man is, what his
powers are, where he stands, and his ultimate fate. It's
the single source that describes God's plan and his Son's
mission to rescue man from the power of the enemy and
to inaugurate a new heaven and a new earth where
there'll be no more tears or pains. It's the exclusive

entrance whereby man can gain a kingdom while escaping a future of endless hellfire and brimstone.

One can't mindlessly shelve the Word next to ragamuffin pseudodoxies of the day and expect to get any results; the gospel has to be seized and swallowed. The Israelites of old swooned over the plagues of frogs, boils, and hail that God used to win them over, but scoffed at his promised land that flowed with milk and honey. Their unbelief left them carcasses in the desert. The Word, not being blended with faith, didn't profit them a lick. And the Nazarenes, who took offense at "The Spirit of the Lord is upon me, for He has anointed me," were left to die in their beds. Esteeming the Word a common book yields the same fruit.

But there were those who deemed it divine; saw it as that pearl of great price and gave up all to have it: the woman with the issue of blood who fought crowds to just touch Jesus; blind Bartamaeus who shouted all the more when Jesus' own disciples tried to quell his cries for mercy; Jairus, the synagogue ruler, who surrendered all—his occupation, his religion, his social life—to heal his daughter; the Canaanite who fought for scraps to have her daughter delivered. And they received the light of life. No one who has esteemed the gospel a God-breathed treasure has ever been left empty-handed.

Healing is the believer's prerogative. "Himself bore my sicknesses and carried away my pains" is inspired truth, to those who blend it with faith. The faithless believer—the one who scoffs at that truth because of the giants he sees in the land—can expect the same results as the Israelites and the Nazarenes that have gone before him. With God, the only currency is faith (Heb 4:6). There is no other.

2

Origins of Sickness and Disease

The Initial Creation

We are used to seeing disease wreak havoc on the most fragile victims; watching little ones suffer the tortures of the damned, wringing our hands as the disease invades and strangles life from their bones, muscles, and organs. That's our world. But it wasn't always that way.

Long ago, God created a world bereft of any disease. Man stood proud as God's ultimate creation, a spiritual being encased in flesh. He breathed into man his own heavenly materiality—the very life of God—so Adam had full range and movement in both the natural order and God's own spiritual dimension. Adam, Eve, and Eden were so pristine that Adam could look upon Eve's nakedness without any hint of shame or humiliation (Gn 2:25). There was no unrighteousness, no death, no decay, and no disease. All was good in the eyes of God.

This picture of purity eludes us because the world, as we've come to know it and live in it, lies in wickedness (1 Jn 5:19 – "the whole world lies in wickedness"). Adam opened the door to disease when he defied God in Eden. Disease is the offspring of what the Word calls sin.

After God created Adam, he gave him one command: Don't eat of the tree of the knowledge of good and evil (Gn 2:7). Why? "Because in the day of your eating, in dying you will die." The edict was terse; Adam would sire spiritual death the moment he sinned. And spiritual death would percolate down through his soul, fingers, and toes rendering pollution and corruption throughout his whole being.

Despite this warning, Adam defied God and ate of the tree. The effect was staggering. Though he retained his spiritual image—the spiritual inner man that was encased with flesh—his conscience and mind were instantly polluted with the taint of spiritual darkness and death (Ti 1:15). He was cankered. Fear seized him. His eyes were opened to darkness; he couldn't look upon Eve, or even himself, without shame, humiliation, and embarrassment (Gn 3:7).

The more expansive revelation of the Gospels show a more graphic picture of Adam's fall. His sin didn't just separate him from God, it ontologically changed his nature. No longer was he a child of God; he was the son of the devil (Jn 8:34; 1 Jn 5:18). And he wasn't a son in name only; he lusted after the devil's own will and desires (Jn 3.34; Eph 2:2-3).

Paul wrote that sin (and its offspring of disease) seized its way to all men when Adam traded away his faith: For this cause, just as through one man, sin into the world entered, and through sin, death, and, so death passed through to all men (Rom 5:12). It was through this plague of sin that disease entered the world. By his sin, Adam became the very offspring of the adversary. And this regeneration permitted the onslaught of disease, which is another form of satanic oppression (Acts 10:38). The root of disease is spiritual. This is borne out in several instances of Jesus' ministry.

Disease: The Sin Connection

In Mark, a paralyzed boy was lowered in front of Jesus by four men who had broken through the roof (Mk 2:1-12). Jesus, addressing the boy, said, "Son, your sins are forgiven." This caused a stir among the scribes: "How can he say that? He blasphemes." Jesus responded, "What's easier to say to this paralyzed boy, Your sins are forgiven; or, Rise up, take up your bed, and walk?"

While the boy no doubt had muscles that wouldn't contract and nerves that wouldn't fire, Jesus didn't address those natural issues. He focused on the spiritual root of the boy's disease. In saying, "Your sins are forgiven," he showed a connection between sin and disease; relieving the burden of sin and healing the sick were one and the same.

Sin as a Causal Link to Disease

The sin link to disease is also shown with the man at the pool of Bethesda (Jn 5:1-9, 14). There, Jesus came upon a man lying on the edge of the pool, hoping to be the first in once the waters were stirred. From time to time, an angel would stir the waters and the first one in the pool would be healed.

When Jesus approached the man, he asked him, "Would you like to be healed?" The man responded, "I don't have anyone to put me in when the waters are stirred." Jesus said, "Rise up! Take up your bed and walk." The man was healed instantly. Sometime later, Jesus ran into him in the temple and said to him, "Look, you're healed. Don't sin anymore lest a worse thing come on you."

His warning is telling. He didn't warn the man about medicinal remedies or the dietary proscriptions of the law. He warned him that any future sin—sin is a spiritual act—could have physical consequences, even worse than he had before. The causal connection between sin and disease is unmistakable.

Healing of the Blind Boy

As Jesus was walking to a village, he came upon a man blind from birth (Jn 9:1-7). His disciples asked, "Master, who sinned, this man or his parents, that he was born blind. Jesus answered them, "Neither this man nor his parents."

The man at the pool of Bethesda shows that sometimes there may be a direct link between a specific sin and disease; but this account demonstrates that isn't always the case. A paraphrase answering the disciples' question of "Who sinned?" might be: "Neither. Disease isn't always tied to some specific sin; the world lies in darkness. Thus men suffer the effects of sin in the world whether they, themselves, sinned or not."

After answering "Neither this man nor his parents sinned," Jesus added: "But the works of God should be manifest in him. I must work the works of him that sent me, while it is day: the night comes when no man can work. As long as I am in the world, I am the light of the world." With that, he spat on the ground, made some clay, and anointed the man's eyes with it. "Go wash in the pool of Siloam." The man did and came out seeing.

Jesus contrasting himself as the light of the world to the man's blindness is noteworthy. By calling himself light, he cast the man's blindness as an outworking of spiritual darkness. Thus, the man's blindness was not the work of God; the work of God was the healing of the disease.

Bent-Over Woman

Perhaps the most graphic example of the sin-disease connection is the bent-over woman of Luke 13. Here, Jesus was teaching in one of the synagogues when he saw a woman who was hunched over—she couldn't stand up straight. He called out to her, "Woman, you're loosed from your disease." Immediately, her back was straightened.

The ruler of the synagogue grumbled that this healing occurred on the sabbath, a day where no work was to be performed (he considered healing work). Jesus responded, "You hypocrite! Doesn't each one of you loose his donkey from the stall to water him on the sabbath? (assume a nodding of heads) And ought not this woman, being a daughter of Abraham, whom Satan hath bound these eighteen years, be loosed from this bond on the sabbath too?"

The Word describes this woman as having a spirit of infirmity. *Infirmity* in the Greek is ἀσθενείας, the most common word for sickness. When Jesus responded to the synagogue ruler, he didn't refer to sickness, but said that Satan had bound her for eighteen years (the Greek word for bound (or bond) is δεσμοῦ which means bond, chain, or imprisoned). A reasonable translation of Jesus' response would be that Satan had imprisoned her for eighteen years.

This woman's story peels back the spiritual underpinnings of disease and shows us that even the most common maladies (spirit of sickness) are manifestations of some sort of demonic oppression (*cf.* Acts 10:38).

While disease may rear its head in petrified tendons, dead nerves, misfiring organs, or cancerous cells, it's rooted in spiritual oppression. The Word shows—in every instance—that disease is the work of spiritual oppression; sin entered the world through Adam and its offspring, disease, arrived with it. And while man, through his doctors and treatments and medicines and therapies, might do his best to thwart its onslaught,

God's real remedy is rooted in the spirit—the finished work of his Son that destroyed Satan's power and domination over those who believe.

3

God's Method of Healing is Spiritual

One of the most striking things about the Word of God toward man's systems of healing is that they are ignored as nonexistent.

Since the root of sickness and disease is spiritual, God's method of healing is spiritual. In Acts 10:38, the Word says that God anointed Jesus with the Holy Ghost and power and, with those, healed all sicknesses and all diseases. It might seem trite, but God didn't give him a medical bag. There's no instance recorded anywhere in the Word where Jesus effected a cure by prescribing some medicinal remedy. Indeed, the very same verse says that all the people's sickness and disease stemmed from a single spiritual source—satanic oppression. God met the spiritual root of disease with his own spiritual remedy.

And while today's preachers tout that doctors are God's tools to effect healing, it's telling that Paul didn't call on Luke, a physician, to support his healing ministry with his medical practice. Indeed, while Luke's medical knowledge has helped us understand certain facts about Jesus' ministry (the sweating of blood, Lk 22:44; and Peter's mother-in-law's *great* fever, Lk 4:38), God's method of healing has always remained grounded in the spirit.

Timothy's Wine

In his first letter to Timothy, Paul instructed the young preacher to "no longer be a water-drinker, but make use of a little wine for your stomach and frequent illnesses" (1 Tm 5:23). Some have used this directive as authority for the proposition that God has approved the use of all kinds of drugs for healing, but that stretches Paul's prescription well beyond its intended meaning.

In contrast to the old covenant Jew, the new testament believer is free with his diet. All food, not just the kosher variety, is sanctified by the word of God and prayer. (1 Tm 4:5 - "For every creature of God is good [for food], and nothing to be refused, if it be received with thanksgiving: for it is sanctified by the word of God and prayer.") But while we may freely eat, that's not to say that everything is good for the body; all things may be permissible, but not everything is beneficial (1 Cor 10:23). Just as gluttony, Christian or non-Christian, will make one fat, a diet short on the necessary vitamins and proteins will make a body weak. Paul's encouragement of adding wine to a water-only diet falls more into the category of advice for nutrition than some redemptive system for physical healing.

Hezekiah's Poultice

Hezekiah, king of the Jews became ill; so ill, in fact, that Isaiah told him that he needed to put his affairs in order because he wasn't going to recover (Is 38). But once Isaiah left, Hezekiah turned his face to the wall and prayed. Hearing his prayer, God instructed Isaiah to go back and tell Hezekiah that, because of his prayer, he would add fifteen years to his life.

Concomitant to this word, Isaiah told Hezekiah's servants to take a lump of figs and lay it "for a plaster on the boil [or carbuncle]" (Is 38:21). Some have tried to transmogrify Isaiah's instruction as some God-approved medical remedy, but that's a misreading. Isaiah had already prophesied that Hezekiah was going to die. It was the answer to Hezekiah's prayer—an added fifteen years—that effected the healing. The figs were not some miracle cure for boils that God suddenly revealed to his prophet; they were a test of obedience in the same pattern as Naaman's dipping in the Jordan seven times (2 Kgs 5:10, 14) and the blind man's washing of Jesus' spittle in the pool of Siloam (Jn 9:6, 7).

James's Anointing Oil

Preachers have also used James's instruction to use anointing oil to pray for the sick as proof of God's use of medicinal remedies for healing. That's another misread because the passage's context shows that it's the prayer of faith and not the oil, that saves or heals the sick one. James writes, "Is any sick among you? let him call for the elders of the church; and let them pray over him, anointing him with oil in the name of the Lord. And the prayer of faith shall save the sick, and the Lord shall raise him up; and if he hath committed sins, they shall be forgiven him" (Jas 5:14-15).

His instruction mirrors the account of Jesus and the paralytic boy. In that account, Jesus said that his imperative to the boy—"Rise up!"—and that his sins were forgiven were essentially the same thing. James, too, says that the sick one's sins would be forgiven in the midst of the prayer of faith—which firmly plants the root of the disease, and its cure, on the spiritual side of things. The oil, by itself, couldn't have anything to do with the forgiveness of sins; it's a symbol of the anointing that Jesus carried with him in his earthly ministry (*see* Acts 10:38) that now has been given to the church (Mk 16:18).

There are those who say that the oil does play a part in healing because James used the word *aleifo*, a word meaning "to besmear," instead of *chiero,* the word ordinarily used to denote anointing (*see* Lk 4:18 – "The Spirit of the Lord is upon me for he has *anointed* me"). But it's a difference without any distinction in meaning. In Exodus, God instructed Moses to anoint Aaron to serve in the office of the high priest (Ex 40:13-15). The Septuagint uses *chiero* for "anoint." But in the same breath, God instructed Moses to anoint Aaron's sons too, and the Septuagint uses *aleifo* for "anoint." Thus, while *chiero* might carry a more sublime meaning, *aleifo* is also used to denote sanctification unto the Lord. We see that in the New Testament where Luke wrote that Mary anointed (*aliefo*) Jesus' feet with oil (Lk 7:46). Unless we were to think that God called on Moses to heal Aaron's sons and that Mary smeared oil on Jesus' ailing feet, there's no reason to believe that James believed that oil effected the sick one's healing.

4

The Old Testament

The Old Covenant

God provided for healing under the old covenant. After he delivered the Israelites from the Egyptians and Moses had led them through the Red Sea, God laid down this proscription:

> If you will diligently hearken to the voice of Yahweh, thy God, and will do that which is right in his eyes, and will give ear to his commandments, and keep all his statutes, I will permit none of the diseases on you, which I have permitted on the Egyptians: for I am Yahweh, who heals you. (Ex 15:26)

Healing wasn't predicated on any kind of divine whimsy; it was available to every man, woman, and child who dared to walk upright before him.

Later, God met with Moses and gave him the Law— what we know as the first five books of the Bible. Moses wrote it down, built an altar, and then had the younger Israelites offer burnt and peace offerings to the Lord. With all the Israelites gathered together, he sprinkled ox blood on the altar and read the Law aloud to them (Heb 9:19). They responded, "All that the Lord has said will we do, and be obedient." Moses took the rest of the blood and sprinkled it on them, saying, "Behold, the blood of the covenant, which the Lord has made with you concerning these words." In the Law, God reaffirmed his first promise of healing to his people: "And you shall serve the Lord, your God, and he shall bless your bread, and your water; and I will take sickness away from the midst of you. There shall nothing cast their young, nor be barren, in thy land: the number of thy days I will fulfill" (Ex 23:25, 26).

Promise in the Promised Land

And when the Israelites, after forty years of wandering the desert for their disbelief, were ready to enter the promised land, God again reiterated his promise. He not only told them that he would take away sickness from their midst, but that the sicknesses would come upon all those that opposed them: And the Lord will take away from thee all sickness, and will permit none of the evil diseases of Egypt, which you know, upon you; but will allow them to lay on all them that hate you (Ex 7:15).

Some might say that God's revelation as Israel's healer ("I am Yahweh Rapha, the Lord that heals you") and his healing promises don't apply to new testament believers because the old covenant has been superseded. True, the old has been taken out of the way to make room for the new, but that doesn't mean that it should be ignored. To the contrary. Israel's deliverance from Egypt, wanderings in the desert for unbelief, and final entry into the promised land are all part of a larger type and shadow of the life of the new testament believer.

In Corinthians, for instance, Paul casts Israel's deliverance through the Red Sea as a type of the new testament believer's baptism into the body of Christ. Later on in the book, he even goes so far as to say that some of the old covenant passages weren't just written for the Jews, but directly for our benefit: "Or says he it altogether for our sakes? For our sakes, no doubt, this is written: 'that he that plows should plow in hope; and that he that threshes in hope should partake in his hope'" (1 Cor 9:10, *quoting* Dt 25:4). The writer of Hebrews also says that the Law, including God's promise of healing, was a shadow of the good things to come under the new covenant (Heb 10:1).

So, while new testament believers aren't under the old covenant, we can look to its promises, types, and shadows to learn of the better promises of our own covenant (Heb 8:6). Through God's covenant with Israel, we see that divine healing is one part of our bundle of redemptive rights in Christ Jesus.

Types and Shadows of Christ's Work

The Old Testament doesn't just show God as Israel's healer. It also contains types and shadows of Jesus' finished work in his death, burial, and resurrection and its provision for healing for all those who believed in and are identified with him.

Aaron's Stay of the Plague

Under the Law, the high priest had special standing because he was the only person who could enter the Holy of Holies of the tabernacle to make atonement for the people. Once a year, on the Day of Atonement, he donned a white linen robe made just for the occasion, took the blood of a sacrificed goat beyond the veil, and sprinkled it on the mercy seat of the ark of the covenant. Only when he did this, and did it exactly right, were Israel's sins atoned or covered.

The writer of Hebrews flatly declares that the Day of Atonement was a type and shadow of Jesus' role as high priest of the new covenant. He also identifies Jesus as the high priest of the new covenant and describes how, on the third day, he entered into the heavenly Holy of Holies and sprinkled his own blood on the ark in heaven. By accomplishing this, he obtained a forever salvation for mankind (Heb 9:12).

Numbers 16 gives us a type and shadow of healing under Jesus' priesthood. The Israelites started murmuring against Moses and Aaron (Israel's high priest) about how the Lord had treated some of the men who had defied them. When Moses stood up before the people to calm them down, the Lord told him to separate himself and Aaron away from them. The moment they did, a plague came on the crowd. Aaron quickly took a censer out and ran into the middle of them, attempting to make atonement for their sin. The Word says that where he stood, he "stood between the dead and the living"; the plague was stayed (Nm 16:48).

Our high priest has not just gone beyond the veil, but has passed through the heavens, and he has made full atonement for us. He stands as Aaron—between those who are oppressed by Satan and those who have been set free into the perfect law of liberty.

The Passover Lamb

After nine plagues had struck Egypt, Moses gave Pharoah an ultimatum: let the children of Israel go or all of Egypt's firstborns, from the lowest to the highest, would die. Pharoah stood his ground and refused to allow the Israelites to leave.

Once Pharoah fated his choice, the Lord told Moses how the Israelites could protect themselves against the plague. Each house was to take an unblemished lamb, kill it, and smear its blood on the front door posts. Then they were to roast its meat, eat it (without breaking any of its bones), and burn any leftovers. They were to make unleavened bread to eat with it because they had to be ready to leave at a moment's notice (they couldn't wait for the yeast to rise). If they did this, the plague would pass over their house (hence the name, *passover lamb*).

On the appointed night, the death angel passed over all the blood-smeared door posts, but struck every other household in Egypt, including Pharoah's. The sorrow in Egypt was so great that Pharoah forced Moses and the

Israelites out before dawn. Psalms says that there wasn't one feeble man, woman, or child that left that night (Ps 105:37); the passover lamb had brought God's healing and strength to all those who ate of it.

When John the Baptist first saw Jesus, he exclaimed, "Behold! the lamb of God who takes away the sin of the world," an obvious reference to the passover lamb. Paul, too, called Christ "our passover" (1 Cor 5:7) and told the Corinthian church that many of them were sick, and some had even died, because they hadn't discerned the benefits of Christ's body and blood (1 Cor 11:27-30).

The Bronze Snake

At one point in the Israelites' wilderness wanderings, Moses sent messengers to the king of Edom, asking for passage through his land. The king responded, "You won't pass here or I'll come at you with a sword." So Israel turned away from Edom and went to Mount Hor.

While there, Arad of the Canaanites sought to fight them. As they were being attacked, they vowed to the Lord: if he delivered the Canaanites into their hands, they'd destroy all the Canaanites' cities. The Lord hearkened unto Israel's vow and delivered Israel from the Canaanites. Israel destroyed all the Canaanite cities (the Lord called the place Hormah, Utter Destruction), but they began grumbling because they had to pass by Edom again.

"Why did you bring us up out of Egypt? to die in the wilderness? There's no water or bread here and we hate manna." Their grumblings and murmurings against the

Lord opened the door for venomous snakes to crawl in among them, biting and killing them.

It wasn't long before they pleaded with Moses: "We've sinned for we've spoken against the Lord. Pray that he take the snakes away from us." Moses prayed and the Lord told him, "Make a fiery snake out of bronze and put it on a pole. Everyone that's been bitten who looks upon that pole will live." Moses did what he said, and every one of the wounded Israelites who looked upon Moses' snake was healed and lived.

In John's Gospel, Jesus analogized his own death, burial, and resurrection to Moses' snake in the desert. He'd been asked, "How can a man be born again?" and he answered, "As Moses lifted up the snake in the desert, so must the son of man be lifted: that whoever believes on him shouldn't perish, but have life eternal." The type of the bronze snake demonstrates that Jesus was to become cursed for us so that everyone who believed on him—looked upon him and identified with him—would live and be healed (*see* Jas 1:25 – whoever looks into the law of liberty shall be blessed in his deed). By becoming sin, he would triumph over the one who had the power of sin and death and provide the remedy for sin's offspring—disease.

The Healing of the Leper

The Law provided for the cleansing (healing) of the leper (Lv 14:1-7). A leper claiming that he had been healed under the Law was to present himself before the priest. If the priest saw that he had been healed, then he'd take two birds and kill one of them in a pot under running water. Then he'd dip the live bird, along with cedar, scarlet, and hyssop into the dead bird's blood and sprinkle the leper seven times with it. He'd pronounce the leper clean, and release the bird to fly away.

The killed bird was a type of Jesus crucified. The live bird—a type of new testament believer—was dipped in the dead bird's blood and anointed with hyssop (*see* Ex 22:22 – hyssop put on the door frame for the passover lamb). Once he was cleansed of all impurities, he was set free (Jn 8:36 – whom the Son sets free is free indeed).

5

Distributions

God's method of healing didn't just consist of his covenant with Israel; it also included distributions of the Holy Ghost (Heb 2:14). Israel's prophets spoke of redemption, of the coming Righteous One who would save mankind, and God confirmed their prophecies with signs, wonders, and these distributions. And, very often, they were manifested in the form of a tangible healing anointing.

Elijah and the Widow in Zarephath

Elijah's first appearance in the Word occurs when he stands before Ahab and announces that it wouldn't rain again in Israel until he gave the order (1 Kgs 17). After giving this dour pronouncement, the Lord told Elijah to hide himself at the brook called Cherith to escape Ahab's anger. After the brook dried up, the Lord told him to go to Zarephath, outside of Israel, and a widow would provide for him there.

While staying with her (with the help of a bottomless cruse of oil), her son contracted an illness and died. She was overwrought, "What have I to do with you? O man of God? Have you come here to call my sins to remembrance and kill my son!?!"

Elijah quietly took the boy's body into a loft upstairs and stretched himself over it three separate times, praying, "O Lord, my God, let this child's soul come into him again." The Lord hearkened and the boy revived (1 Kgs 17:22). After receiving back her boy, the woman said, "Now I know you are a man of God, and God's word is in your mouth."

This account demonstrates some nuances of the healing anointing. First, Elijah didn't put God in remembrance of his covenant with Israel (that he'd take sickness from the midst of them) because the widow and her son weren't Israelites (the widow's son's healing was effected by faith in the prophet's declaration of the coming Redeemer) (see Lk 4:22-27). Second, he stretched his body out on the boy's body not just once, but three different times. Why? By stretching himself out upon the boy, Elijah maximized the anointing's coverage as he much as he could. And, by lying on him three times, he compounded its action and effects.

Elisha and the Shunammite's Son

Elisha occasionally stayed with a woman from Shumen and her husband during his ministry travels. Elisha saw them so often, in fact, that they constructed a small bedroom for him to stay in when he came to visit.

One day, while Elisha was staying with them, he asked the woman, "You've done all this for me, what can I do for you?" She said that she was content, but Gehazi, Elisha's servant, spoke up for her, saying, "She doesn't have a child, and her husband is old." Elisha prophesied that she would conceive within the year and she did. She gave birth to a son.

The boy grew up and, one day when he was working with his father, his head seized up with pain. His father quickly put his work down and took him over to his mother, but he soon died in her lap.

She put her son's body on Elisha's bed and she set out to find Elisha. She found him on Mount Carmel with Gehazi. When she met him, she fell at his feet, saying, "Did I ask for a son from you? Didn't I say, 'Don't mislead me?'" and told him that her son had died.

Elisha turned to Gehazi and said, "Take my staff and lay it on the boy." But that wasn't good enough for the Shunammite: "As God lives and you live, I won't leave you!" So Elijah agreed to follow her back to her house.

Gehazi went ahead of both of them. He came to the house, went into the little bedroom and laid Elisha's staff on the boy. Nothing happened.

Elijah arrived and he put both Gehazi and the woman out of the room. He went over to the boy's body and, just like Elijah had done with Zarephath's widow's boy, he laid down on him. He *put his mouth upon his mouth, and his eyes upon his eyes, and his hands upon his hands.* As he transmitted the healing anointing, the body waxed warm and the boy revived.

The Gospels and the New Testament

This healing anointing also rested on Jesus and Paul, both of whom were prophets (Mk 6:4; Acts 13:1). In Mark's gospel, Jesus was heading toward Jairus's house to heal his daughter when a woman with an issue of blood touched him. Immediately he felt the anointing power flow out of him (Mk 5:3), the same power that rest on both Elijah and Elisha (*see* Lk 4:18 – "The Spirit of the Lord is upon me, for he has anointed me."). People recognized this anointing on Paul because they took his work aprons and handkerchiefs from him and laid them on the sick and the possessed. The anointing, transmitted into the cloths, cured diseases and even cast out demons (Acts 19:12).

Peter apparently had this anointing, too, because people laid the sick out in the streets just hoping that his shadow might pass over them, healing them (Acts 5:15). His shadow wasn't the healing agent, it was the anointing resting upon him that was so strong that people thought they just had to get close to him to be healed (*compare* Jn 18:6 – Jesus says, "I am he" and the Roman soldiers fell out backwards under the power of the Spirit).

The Healing Anointing Fluxes

The Word not only evidences the fact of the healing anointing, but how it fluxes in strength and on faith. Once Elisha learned of the Shunammite's boy's death, he told Gehazi to lay his staff on the body, thinking that his staff, having enough residual anointing in it by virtue of his own contact with it (compare Paul's aprons), would carry enough of the anointing to revive the boy. Apparently it didn't. This particular sickness required a stronger measure. It required the full measure of the prophet's distribution and that, three separate times (*compare* 2 Kgs 13:20-21 – soldier revived after just touching Elisha's bones).

Jesus healed the woman with the issue of blood instantly through a transference of the anointing, but could only heal a few minor ailments in Nazareth through the laying on of hands because they refused to believe his message (Mk 6:5). In another instance, he had to lay his hands on a man twice—intensifying the anointing's power—to fully heal a man's eyes (Mk 8:22-25).

While the healing anointing might rest on a particular preacher, even strongly (*see* Jn 6:34 – Jesus was given the Spirit *without measure*), its ability to effect a cure fluxes not only by the strength of the distribution, but also on the faith of the ones seeking to receive of it (*see* Lk 4:25, 26 – Jesus compares the many widows in Israel to the one in Zarephath).

Charismata – Gifts of the Spirit

Concomitant to the healing anointing, God confirmed the Word with signs and wonders. In 1 Corinthians 12, Paul catalogs the different kinds of *spirituals* or manifestations of the Holy Ghost given and administered as the Lord directs. They include the working of miracles, gifts of healings, the word of knowledge, and the word of wisdom. These gifts aren't exclusive to the church age, but were in operation under the old covenant, too (except for tongues and the interpretation of tongues).

In contrast to the healing anointing, these manifestations don't operate on the basis of transference or proximity. They come about only as the Lord wills (1 Cor 12:11 – distributing to each one even as he is disposed). Thus, a preacher can't exercise faith for them to operate, but, with that in mind, they're manifested more regularly with someone who has been doused with a distribution of the Holy Ghost than with others. That is why prophets under the old covenant weren't viewed only as seers, or foretellers, but also healers (*see* 2 Kgs 5:3 – "Would to God there was a prophet in Samaria! for he would recover him from his leprosy."). Normally, the different gifts are manifested in combination to effect a cure.

Naaman's Leprosy

Naaman was a great military commander, but he was a Samaritan and a leper. After a military campaign, the Syrians took some Israelites captive and Naaman took one of the girls to work as a mistress to his wife. One day, seeing that he was a leper, she said to Naaman's wife, "Would to God that there was a prophet in Samaria! for he would recover him of his leprosy." With that, Syria's king dispatched a letter to Israel's king, asking him to cure Naaman of his leprosy. The king was flummoxed:

"Am I God, to kill and make alive? that this king asks me to heal Naaman of his leprosy?"

When Elisha heard about it, he sent word that the king should send Naaman over to him so "he shall know that there is a prophet in Israel."

Naaman got word of Elisha's message and led his entourage over to Elisha's house. Gehazi, Elisha's servant, met him at the door and told him that Elisha had said that if he would wash seven times in the Jordan, he'd be healed.

Naaman was infuriated; he had wanted Elisha to lay hands on him. Dip in the Jordan? "Aren't the rivers in Damascus better than anything in Israel? Why can't I bathe in those?" He stormed off to his chariot, but his servants finally cajoled him into following Elisha's instructions ("What do you have to lose?"). So he rode to the Jordan, dipped seven times, and his skin was made as fresh as a baby's. He went back to Elisha's house, saying, "I know that there is no God in the earth, except God in Israel."

Before heading off to Elisha's house, Naaman might have investigated and heard of the Shunammite widow's boy. He was apparently aware of Elisha's healing anointing because he wanted Elisha to "take his stand, and call on the name of Yahweh, and wave his hand towards the spot." But Elisha didn't touch him. In fact, he didn't even meet him at the door. Elisha, instead, gave him specific instructions of what to do to be healed—a manifestation of a word of wisdom (dip in the Jordan seven times) and of the gifts of healings and miracles (healing of the leprosy and creation of new skin). These manifestations converted Naaman to the Word.

The Blind Man and the Pool of Siloam

The charismata operated in Jesus' earthly ministry the same way. Once, as Jesus and his disciples were passing by a man blind from birth, Jesus stopped to heal him without any preaching (Jn 9:1-9). He spat on the ground, made clay of the spittle, and anointed the man's eyes with it. Then he told the man to wash his eyes in the pool of Siloam and he'd be healed. The man did and came out seeing.

If the healing anointing had been used to heal the man's blindness—like the blind man in Mark 8—Jesus wouldn't have spat on the ground or given the man any idiosyncratic instructions. He would have laid his hands on him for the transfer of the healing anointing, and the anointing would have effected the cure. Here, the charismata were in operation. No preaching or laying on of hands was needed. The man received his healing very much like Naaman received his—obeying the manifestation of a word of wisdom and gifts of healing that had come through God's prophet.

Both Hebrews and Corinthians show that these spiritual distributions and charismata didn't end with Jesus' ministry, but were meant to continue to confirm the Word through the church age. In Hebrews, the writer said that in ages past God had spoken through the prophets and bore witness with them. He goes on to say that God has spoken through his Son and that he continues to bear witness of his gospel with signs, wonders, divers miracles, and distributions of the Holy Ghost (Heb 2:4 – bearing witness (*sunepimarturountos*) being a present active participle). In the same vein, Paul wrote that the Lord wouldn't cease administering the gifts until that which is perfect—the full redemption of the sons of God—has come (1 Cor 13:10).

6

Jesus' Spiritual Distribution

How God Anointed Jesus

Many preach that the miracles and healings that Jesus performed were to prove his divine nature. They're wrong. When Jesus accepted the Father's mission to save man from the ravages of sin, he emptied himself of all his preincarnate glory (Phil 2:6, 7 – he emptied (*ekenōsen -* ἐκένωσεν) himself). By using *ekenōsen*, Paul emphasizes that it was every last drop. So when Jesus was born in Bethlehem, God had to anoint him like he did the old covenant prophets (Jn 5:19 – the son can do nothing of himself). That's why Jesus didn't heal anyone before he was baptized in the Jordan river.

When it was time for Jesus to enter his ministry, he asked John (the Baptizer) to baptize him. At first, John refused: "I need to be baptized by you and you're coming to me?" (Mt 3:14). But Jesus implored him, "Permit it because it behooves us to fulfill all righteousness" (Mt 4:15). John consented, and as Jesus came up out of the water, he saw the heavens rip back like a scroll and the Spirit descend on Jesus like a dove (Mt 3:16).

This was Jesus' anointing for ministry—a spiritual distribution from heaven where he could effect healings and become a conduit for the gifts of the Spirit. It was an anointing *without measure* (Jn 3:34). After Jesus endured his testing in the desert, he returned in the power of the spirit, announcing everywhere he went: "The Spirit of the Lord is upon me, for he has anointed me to preach the gospel to the poor; he has sent me to heal the broken-hearted, to preach deliverance to the captives, and recovering of sight to the blind, and to set at liberty those that are bruised" (Lk 4:18, 19).

Luke limned the spiritual significance of Jesus' Jordan experience: "How God anointed him with Holy Spirit and with power, who penetrated through, doing good, and healing all oppressed by the adversary, because God was with him." Luke compounded the words *kata* (κατα), meaning *down* or *under* and *dunasteuomenos* (δυναστευομένους), meaning *I hold power over* or *I dominate* to derive "oppressed" (καταδυναστευομένους). He wrote it as a present tense participle that is better translated "being continuously dominated." From this, we understand that all the diseases that Jesus healed involved some type of continual Satanic oppression or domination.

What's equally clear from Luke's inspired description is that disease is neither God's will nor his act. His *healing all oppressed* shows that there wasn't a single case that Jesus wasn't willing to heal because God had brought it about; all of them, one way or another, were the work of the adversary. And this wasn't just the case where the demons cried out; it included everyone, even those who suffered what we consider to be organic diseases. He healed them all; the Word doesn't discriminate:

- And Jesus went about all Galilee, teaching in their synagogues, and preaching the gospel of the kingdom, and healing all manner of sickness and all manner of disease (θεραπεύτων πᾶσαν νόσον) among the people. And his fame went throughout all Syria: and they brought unto him all sick people that were taken with divers diseases and torments (τοὺς κακῶς ἔχοντας ποικίλαις νόσοις καὶ Βασάνοις), and those which were possessed with devils, and those which were lunatic, and those that had the palsy; and *he healed them* (ἐθεράπευσεν αὐτούς). (Mt 4:23-24)

- When the even was come, they brought unto him many that were possessed with devils: and he cast out the spirits with his word, and *healed all* (ἐθεράπευσεν πάντας) that were sick. (Mt 8:16)

- And he came down with them, and stood in the plain, and the company of his disciples, and a great multitude of people out of all Judea and Jerusalem, and from the sea coast of Tyre and Sidon, which came to hear him, and to be healed of their diseases (οἱ ἦλθον ἀκοῦσαι αὐτοῦ καὶ ἰσθῆναι ἀπὸ τῶν νόσων αὐτῶν); And they that were vexed with unclean spirits: and *they were healed* (ἰᾶτο πάντας). (Lk 6:17-19)

It's important to note that Jesus met every disease, without exception, with the anointing—the Holy Spirit (his gifts or operations) and spiritual power. He never sought to heal anyone by medicinal means. This was true from blind Bartimaeus whom he told, "Go your way; your faith has made you whole," to Lazarus whom he raised after being dead four days, to everyone besieged by any kind of disease who sought to be healed (Mt 9:35 – and Jesus went about healing every sickness and every disease among the people).

Case Study: The Lunatic Boy

As Jesus was walking down from the mount of transfiguration, he met a crowd arguing with his disciples (Mk 9:14-27). They had tried to heal a boy, but to no effect. The boy's father turned to Jesus, pleading, "Please help my boy. I asked your disciples to heal him, but they could not. He has a speechless spirit that takes him, tears him, and throws him into the fires and into the waters. He foams at the mouth and gnashes his teeth." It appears that his son suffered from grand mal seizures: without showing any initial symptoms, the person falls to the ground, his body stiffens, and his muscles begin to jerk and spasm.

Though the father's description could lend support to a natural diagnosis (he believed that a spirit was behind it), Jesus confronted the condition at its spiritual root.

He didn't ascribe the boy's plight to natural causes or meet the problem with a natural remedy. He rebuked the spirit that was acting behind the symptoms: "You dumb and deaf spirit, come out of him and don't enter into him again!" His rebuke eradicated the demonic oppression, healing the boy.

Case Study: The Blind, Mute Man

In Matthew 12, some people brought a man who was blind and mute for Jesus to heal. In healing him (ἐθεράπευσεν), Jesus laid his hands on the man and cast a devil out (Mt 12:22). Thus, while the man suffered what some might characterize as one or more organic medical illnesses (they weren't psychosomatic), a spiritual personality was actually directly affecting both his eyes and vocal cords.

Degrees of Sickness and Oppression

While Acts 10:38 illuminates satanic oppression as the real root of disease, that's not to say that all those who are sick are possessed by demons. Much illness germinates because "the whole world lies in wickedness" (1 Jn 5:19) due to the fall. For instance, when Jesus went to Nazareth, he was able to cure a few with just minor ailments. The Word doesn't evidence the presence of demon spirits, so we may assume that none were present. The same is true for Peter's mother-in-law's fever. Jesus rebuked the fever (ἐπετίμησεν τῷ πυρετῷ – *rebuked the fever*), not any personality behind it (see Lk 4:39).

41

In contrast to the Nazarenes or Peter's mother-in-law was the madman of Gadera (Mk 5:1-17; Lk 8:26-27). This man had been fully possessed for a long time. The demons had turned him into a sadist—he cut himself with stones for gratification. The possession didn't affect just his mind, but his nerves, ligaments, tendons, and muscles; he was able to break chains, fetters, and bands with his bare hands. No one could hold him. And when he spoke, the possessing demon controlled his tongue and vocal cords (Lk 8:28 – "What have I do to with you, Jesus, Son of the Most High? I beg you. Don't torment me."). Spiritual oppression can run the gamut—from the mildest fever all the way to full-blown demonic possession where the demons affect and control a man's mind and biology—but the remedy remained the same: the Holy Ghost and power.

Jesus' Attitude Toward Sickness

Jesus never met a disease with kindness. And he never acted as though sickness were God's will. He had the same brusque attitude and used the same harsh rebuke, *epitamaō* (ἐπιταμάω), for sickness as he did for evil spirits.

Once, he was teaching in the synagogue when a demon-possessed man blurted out, "Leave us alone! what have we to do with you, Jesus of Nazareth? Have you come to destroy us? I know who you are: the Holy One of God" (Lk 4:30-35). Jesus immediately rebuked (*epetimēsen* – ἐπετιμησεν) the spirit: "Shut up! and come out of him!" The devil tore the man, but then he came out.

Shortly after this (*see* Lk 1:3 – Luke's gospel is chronological), Peter invited Jesus to his house. When Jesus came in, he found that Peter's mother-in-law lay bedridden with a severe fever. Peter and the other disciples asked him to heal her. He went over to her bed, stood over her, and rebuked the fever the same way he did the spirit in the synagogue (Lk 4:39 - ἐπετίμησεν τῷ πυρετῷ – *rebuked the fever*). His attitude towards this indirect oppression—a demon-free sickness—was no different from those whose oppression was direct:

- And Jesus *rebuked* (*epetimēsen* – ἐπετιμησεν) the devil; and he departed out of him: and the child was cured from that very hour. (Mt 17:18)

- And the impure spirits, as soon as they beheld him, were falling down to him, and crying aloud, while he was speaking, You are the Son of God! and sternly was he rebuking them (*epitima* – ἐπετίμα), lest they should make him known. (Mk 3:11-12)

- And devils also came out of many, crying out, and saying, Thou art Christ the Son of God. And he *rebuking* (*epitimōn* – ἐπιτιμῶν) them suffered them not to speak: for they knew that he was the Christ. (Lk 4:41)

If disease were God's will, as some suggest, Jesus wouldn't have rebuked Peter's mother-in-law's fever the same way that he did these demons.

Two Problematic Translations

Two new testament accounts are often used for the proposition that God creates sickness for the devout believer. The two are the man born blind (Jn 9:1-7) and the story of Lazarus (Jn 11:1-44).

The Blind Man

The blind man's account:

> As He passed by, He saw a man blind from birth. And His disciples asked Him, "Rabbi, who sinned, this man or his parents, that he would be born blind?" Jesus answered, "It was neither that this man sinned, nor his parents; *but it was so that* the works of God might be displayed in him. We must work the works of Him who sent Me as long as it is day; night is coming when no one can work. While I am in the world, I am the Light of the world." When He had said this, He spat on the ground, and made clay of the spittle, and applied the clay to his eyes, and said to him, "Go, wash in the pool of Siloam" (which is translated, Sent). So he went away and washed, and came back seeing. (NASB)

The NASB (and the ESV) translate the *hina* (ἵνα) clause (*but it was so that*) as a subordinate conjunction, describing why the man was born blind. True, it should be translated that way most of the time. But translating it that way here makes Jesus look like he is play-acting—God has used Satan to create the man's blindness just so Jesus could come and heal him, so God could be "glorified."

The better translation treats *hina* (ἵνα) as an imperative.[1] That translation looks like this:

> As He passed by, He saw a man blind from birth. And His disciples asked Him, "Rabbi, who sinned, this man or his parents, that he would be born blind?" Jesus answered, "Neither that this man sinned, nor his parents. . . . But the works of God should be manifest in him! We must work the works of Him who sent Me as long as it is day; night is coming when no one can work. While I am in the world, I am the Light of the world."

Here, the *hina* clause is connected to Jesus doing the works of God, not the origin of the man's blindness. In response to the disciples' question, Jesus doesn't dwell on how the man became blind, but on how he can effect the works of God to cure him. It's not only

---

[1] Compare other *hina* imperatives: Col 2:4 ("What I mean is this: Nobody is to talk you round . . ."); Jn 14:31 ("the world needs to learn"); Jn 1:8 ("he had to bear witness").

grammatically correct, it's scripturally accurate. It's also consistent with Acts 10:38—disease is the work of the adversary and God anointed Jesus to break that oppression. This translation and the balance of scripture proves that God isn't the author of disease, Satan is.

Lazarus

In John 11, Lazarus contracted an illness and his sisters sent word to Jesus. When the message was relayed to him, he said, "This sickness is not unto death, but for the glory of God, that the Son of God might be glorified thereby" (Jn 11:4, King James Version).

The usual take on this is that Lazarus contracted a terminable illness as part of God's overall plan to glorify his son. Like the misconstrued translation of the blind man's account, God fated Lazarus to become sick just so Jesus could come along, raise him from the dead, and show everyone that God is the giver *and taker* of life. This interpretation is hinged on the conjunction *but* (ἀλλα) and preposition *for* (ὑπερ): This sickness isn't unto death, *but for* God's glory.

But Greek words, like their English counterparts, usually don't have just one meaning. They communicate different nuances depending on context (and some nuances are theologically-driven). *Alla* (Αλλα), for instance, is usually translated *but* because it can mark a contrast from one idea to the next. But that's not its only meaning. In John 16.2, it's used to give emphasis, not contrast: "They will put you out of the synagogues: *yea* (ἀλλα), the time comes, that whoever kills you will think that he's doing God a service." In 2 Corinthians 7:11, it's used to convey an accessory idea:

> For behold this selfsame thing, that you
> sorrowed after a godly sort,
>> what carefulness it wrought in you,
>> *yea* (αλλα), what clearing of yourselves,
>> *yea* (αλλα), what indignation,
>> *yea* (αλλα), what fear,
>> yea (αλλα), what vehement desire,
>> *yea* (αλλα), what zeal,
>> *yea* (αλλα), what revenge!
> In all things ye have approved yourselves to be
> clear in this matter.

And in Romans 15:20-21, it doesn't carry any contrast at all. If anything, it just marks an underlying reason: "Yea, so have I strived to preach the gospel, not where Christ was named, lest I should build upon another man's foundation: *but* (άλλα) as it is written, To whom he was not spoken of, they shall see: and they that have not heard shall understand."

The same thing goes for *hūper*(ὑπερ). Even its primary definition carries all kinds of nuances: *for, in behalf of, for the sake of someone*. And most of the popular Bible translations translate it this way: "Lazarus' sickness was orchestrated for the sake of God's glory." But it can also be causal: "The disciples rejoiced that they were counted worthy to suffer shame *because* (*hūper*) of Jesus' name" (Acts 5:41); "Paul was pleased in infirmities, in reproaches, in necessities, in persecutions, etc., *because* (*hūper*) of Christ" (2 Cor 12:10).

Applying these nuanced uses to Jesus' response, we get: "This sickness won't result in death because of the glory of God, and the son of man will be glorified because of it." Jesus wasn't speaking about why Lazarus became ill; he was saying why it wouldn't end in death —the anointing would eradicate the oppression.

7

Aspects of the Power

The power manifested predominantly in the form of a healing anointing—a tangible power that effected healings and deliverances through transference—and this was the primary way that Jesus ministered healing in his ministry. He'd go from town to town, teaching and preaching Isaiah's prophecy—the Spirit of the Lord was upon him for he had anointed him—and then he'd lay his hands on the sick, healing them of all kinds of diseases and sicknesses (Lk 4:40 – he laid his hands on every one of them and healed them).

Still the Need for Faith

While this power rested on him continually, he couldn't (and didn't) just lay his hands on people indiscriminately. Faith was needed to draw that power out. Without it, he couldn't effect a cure; the power fluxed in relation to faith.

One woman had had a blood hemorrhage for twelve years, spent all that she had on every doctor she could find and not only didn't get better, she got worse (Mk 5:25-30). When she heard about Jesus (apparently someone had told her about his message that the Spirit of the Lord was upon him), she thought to herself, "If I just touch his clothes [with that anointing on him], I'll be healed." And with that, she got out of her sick bed and fought her way through the crowds to get to him.

When she was finally close enough to touch him—and she did touch him—he whizzed around, asking, "Who touched me?" He had felt the power go out of him. And she felt it within herself; it healed her hemorrhage instantly. After hearing her story, Jesus told her, "Your faith has healed you."

Mark's account shows that the throng around Jesus was so tight that the disciples laughed when he turned around asking, "Who touched my clothes?" They said, "You see the crowd thronging you? and you ask, 'Who touched me?'" (ha ha ha). So, while many might have brushed up against him or bumped him, none had reached out in faith. And the power didn't go anywhere. But when she reached out to touch him, thinking that's all she had to do to be healed, her faith unleashed the power, which immediately dissolved the hemorrhage after twelve hard years of suffering.

Later in his gospel, Mark recounts Jesus' visit to his hometown of Nazareth. There, the people didn't seek to touch his robe or even want to hear what he had to say. They were offended at him and derided him: "Where did he come up with these ideas? What is this wisdom that's been given to him? Isn't he the son of that [lowly] carpenter?" Jesus responded by pointing to the widow in Zarephath and Naaman, the leper; telling them, in effect, that their unbelief—their rejection of his message— would thwart the power. They didn't budge. He was taken aback by their unbelief and couldn't (not: *wouldn't*) do more than heal a few of some minor ailments. Their lack of faith had choked the flow so he had to leave those with serious maladies as he found them.

Tangible and Residual Power

The woman with the hemorrhage story highlights certain aspects of the power—its tangibility and ability to be transmitted.

When she finally got through the crowds and reached out to touch Jesus, he wasn't aware of her. He hadn't met her, wasn't talking to her, wasn't praying for her, or even looking to lay his hands. He had set out, making his way through a crowd, to heal a little girl that was next to death (Mk 5:22-24). He was totally oblivious to the woman's plight and her mission to touch him.

But when she touched his robe, he felt it immediately: "Somebody touched me! I felt power come out of me!" (Lk 9:46). And so did she: "and she felt in her body that she was healed of the plague" (Mk 5:29). It wasn't an ephemeral emotion; the power was perceptible to touch—tangible and tactile.

Jesus' surprise—the transmission of power out from him without his foreknowledge or direct control—

shows that the power was always residually present to heal; it just had to be triggered by the touch of faith: "And the whole multitude sought to touch him because power was coming out from him and he was healing all" (Lk 6:19).

Transmittable

The anointing wasn't tangible, but it was transmittable, and not just to the sick or demon-possessed. At least twice in his ministry, Jesus deputized his disciples with the power to expand his own work. The first time, he called his twelve and gave them power—the same word used in Acts 10:38—over devils and to cure diseases (Lk 9:1-2; Mt 10:5-8). Mark reports that they took the power and cast out devils and healed the sick (Mk 6:12).

After this success, Jesus called together seventy more (Lk 10:1). Like the twelve, he told them to heal the sick and then sent them out two-by-two. After conducting their campaign, they came back rejoicing that "even the devils are subject to us through your name." Their commission to heal and their testimony about the devils being subject to them shows how Jesus' own anointing had been tangibly transmitted to them.

It could also be absorbed into certain inanimate objects. When the Shunammite woman sought Elisha about her dead boy, he wanted Gehazi to take his walking staff and lay it on the boy. He recognized the power's tangible properties and knew that some of it had rubbed off on to the staff that he carried with him daily.

The same thing happened in Paul's ministry. Paul worked as a leather crafter during his ministry and his work aprons and handkerchiefs absorbed the power as he worked during the week. People took his aprons and cloths to the sick; the power resident in them healed the sick and even cast out devils (Acts 19:11, 12).

In Jesus' ministry, the woman with the hemorrhage wasn't alone in knowing about its transmittable properties. Everywhere Jesus went, people looked to touching his robe, knowing that it was infused with the power:

- And when they were gone over, they came into the land of Gennesaret. And when the men of that place had knowledge of him, they sent out into all the county round about, and brought unto him all that were diseased; And besought him that they might only touch the hem of his garment: and as many as touched were made perfectly whole. (Mt 14:34-36)

- And whithersoever he entered, into villages, or cities, or country, they laid the sick in the streets, and besought him that they might touch if it were but the border of his garment: and as many as touched him were made whole. (Mk 6:56)

The Power Extended

The power not only rested in his touch, but also in Jesus' word. When Judas betrayed him, he knew that Jesus had often slipped away to the garden of Gethsemene with his disciples to rest from the ministry. So he led the Roman guards there. When they came into the garden with their lanterns and weapons, Jesus asked them, "Who are you looking for?" They said, "Jesus of Nazareth." Jesus responded, saying, "I am he," and when he did, all the soldiers, and the priests and Pharisees with them, fell down backwards (Jn 18:6). His words carried so much of the anointing that they couldn't stand in the face of it (cf. 1 Kgs 8:11; 2 Chr 5:14).

While Jesus healed primarily through the laying on of his hands, he sometimes just used the word of his power. For instance, one night, people brought to him many who were possessed with demons. He cast the demons out with his word (Mt 8:16) while he laid his hands on others (Lk 4:40, 41). In another instance, a centurion soldier asked him to come heal his servant. His servant was sick of the palsy and in a lot of pain. When Jesus said, "I'll come and heal him," the soldier said, "No, wait! All you have to do is say the word and he'll be healed." Jesus did—"Go your way; and as you've believed, so will it be done to you—and his servant was healed that hour (Mt 8:5-13). Jesus effected a healing the same way for a nobleman, healing his son by saying, "Go your way, your son lives" (Jn 4:46-53); and ten lepers who needed cleansing (Lk 17:14 - "Go show yourselves to the priests"). They all had approached him in faith, which triggered the power in the form of an anointed word.

Gateway to the Gifts of the Spirit

The descending of the Spirit at the Jordan also provided Jesus the platform for operating in the gifts of the Spirit (*cf.* Jn 1:33, 2:11). This included the gifts of healings. These gifts weren't triggered by the hearer's faith but were manifested when the Spirit decided (1 Cor 12:11).

An example of this is the man at the pool of Bethesda (Jn 5:2-9). There was a multitude of blind, crippled, and diseased people lying around the edges of the pool, waiting for the stirring of the waters. From time to time, an angel would descend and stir the waters and the first one in the pool would be healed.

This particular man had been infirm for at least thirty-eight years when Jesus walked up to him and asked, "Do you want to be healed?" The man looked up at him and said, "Sir, I don't have a man to put me in the pool. When the water is stirred, someone always gets to the water before me." Without more, Jesus told him, "Get up! Take up your bed and walk." Instantly the man was healed.

The gifts of healing had manifested. The man didn't hear a message. He didn't hear that Jesus had been anointed—that he had been sent to preach deliverance to the captives and recovery of sight to the blind. None of the multitude sought to touch him or his robe. The Spirit had sovereignly acted to effect this man's healing, which affirmed Jesus' ministry and word (*see* Jn 5:16-18 – "My father works and so do I.").

Jesus had a similar manifestation occur with a blind man that he ran into, between villages. He told his disciples that the works of God should be made manifest in the man, but he didn't preach to him. Instead he dropped to his knees, spat in the dirt and made some clay out of the spittle. He took the spittle and rubbed it on the man's eyes, telling him to wash in the pool of Siloam. The man made his way to the pool and came away seeing. In this instance, Jesus didn't heal the man through the transference of a healing anointing, but it was an idiosyncratic manifestation of the gifts of healing similar to Elisha's healing of Naaman.

8

He Bore Our Diseases

When Jesus drained himself of glory, it wasn't just to heal a multitude or bring the gifts of the Spirit to a few. He took on the form of a servant to destroy the work of the adversary—the spiritual death that spawned a fallen race fraught with cancers, viruses, germs, and palsies. The old testament types—the snake on the pole, the passover lamb, Aaron's censer, the leper's cleansing—all whispered his stout mission: he would become our sin and sickness so we could be healed (2 Cor 5:21).

He'd offer himself on a cross (Heb 9:26, 10:12). There, God would lay on him the sins of us all; he'd fully identify with the fallen men he sought to save. He'd die, cut off from his people, cast off from his God. He'd bear this bruise until every man, every woman, and every child could be healed of the disease—those Satanic oppressions—that spiritual death had wrought against them.

The prophet Isaiah lived some 600 years before Christ, but he saw this. He didn't see the cross like the other gospel writers did, with its beatings, robe, crown of thorns, and nails. He saw the more horrific side. He saw a white lamb led out to his slaughter. He saw how we despised him, mocked him, and turned our faces away in disgust. And he saw how God crushed him and made him sick. All for us.

He wrote:

> Despised was he and forsaken of men,
> Man of pains, and familiar with sickness,—
> Yea like one from whom the face is hidden
> Despised, and we esteemed him not.
>
> Yet surely our sicknesses he carried,
> And, as for our pains, he bore the burden
> of them,—
> But we accounted him stricken
> Smitten of God, and degraded.
>
> Yet he was pierced for transgressions that
> were ours,
> Was crushed for iniquities that were ours,—
> The chastisement for our well-being was
> upon him,
> And by his bruise there is healing for us.

We all like sheep had gone astray,
Every man to his own way, we had turned,
And Yahweh caused to light upon him
The sins of us all.
(Is 53:3-5, *variant* of Rotherham)

We know that he wrote this about Jesus because of
Luke. Luke wrote about an Ethiopian eunuch who was
reading these words while riding in his chariot on his
way back home (Acts 8:26-35). The angel of the Lord
appeared to Philip, the evangelist, and told him to go to
the eunuch's caravan and "join yourself to that chariot."
When he caught up to the chariot, he heard the eunuch
reading Isaiah (they read aloud in those days).
"Understand what you're reading?" "How can I, except
somebody guide me?" He took Philip into his chariot
and continued on: "He was led as a sheep to the
slaughter; and like a lamb dumb before his shearer, so
opened he not his mouth: In his humiliation his
judgment was taken away: and who shall declare his
generation? for his life is taken from the earth." The
eunuch asked, "Who's the prophet speak about? himself,
or someone else?" Starting there, Philip preached Jesus
to him (Acts 8:35).

Familiar with Sickness

Isaiah saw him familiar with sickness. The Righteous
One tasted it, experienced it, and suffered for it. He used
choli for *sickness*, a common word for physical disease:

- And the Lord will take away from thee all *sickness*; and he will put none of the evil diseases of Egypt, which thou knowest upon thee, but will lay them upon all them that hate thee. (Dt 7:15)

- Then the Lord will make thy plagues wonderful, and the plagues of thy seed, even great plagues, and of long continuance, and sore *sicknesses* of long continuance. (Dt 28:59)

- Also every *sickness*, and every plague, which is not written in the book of this law, them will the Lord bring upon thee, until thou hast been destroyed. (Dt 28:61)

- And it came to pass after these things, that the son of the woman, the mistress of the house, fell sick; and his *sickness* was so sore, that there was no breath left in him. (1 Kgs 17:17)

- And Ahaziah fell down through the lattice in his upper chamber that was in Samaria, and was sick: and he sent messengers, and said to them, Go, inquire of Baal-zebub the god of Ekron whether I shall recover this *sickness*. (2 Kgs 1:2)

- And the king said unto Hazael, Take a present in thine hand, and go meet the man of God, and inquire of the Lord by him, saying, Shall I recover of this *sickness*? (2 Kgs 8:8)

- And in the thirty and ninth year of his reign Asa was diseased in his feet; his disease was exceeding great: yet in his *disease* he sought not to the Lord, but to the physicians. (2 Chr 16:12)

- And thou shalt have great *sickness* by disease of thy bowels, until thy bowels fall out by reason of the *sickness*, day by day. (2 Chr 21:15)

- When Ephraim saw his *sickness*, and Judah saw his wound, then went Ephraim to Assyria, and sent to king Jareb: but he is not able to heal you, neither shall he cure you from your wound. (Hos 5:13)

By bearing within himself the root of our diseases (if sickness wasn't spiritual, he couldn't have borne it), he became a man of pains (*makob*). *Makob* is the pains resulting from disease: "Or he is chastised with *pain* on his bed; and the strife of his bones is unceasing" (Jb 33:19).

Borne and Carried

Jesus not only bore our sicknesses and their concomitant agonies, but he took them away from us. In *Yet surely our sicknesses he carried*, Isaiah wrote *nasa* for *carried,* which means to bear in the sense of suffering a punishment. Moses used it in Leviticus for sin and Isaiah did, too:

- When a person sins, in that he hears a public curse against one who fails to testify and he is a witness (he either saw or knows what happened) and he does not make it known, then he will bear (*nasa*) his punishment for iniquity. (Lv 5:1 NET Bible)

- Therefore will I give him a portion in the great, and the strong shall he apportion as spoil because he poured out to death his soul, and with the transgressors let himself be numbered,—Yea he the sin of many bare (*nasa*), and for transgressors interposeth. (Is 53:12 Rotherham)

And he used *sabal* for *bore* in *he bore the burden of pains*. *Sabal* means to bear or undertake a load. Isaiah used it in other places:

- Even unto old age I am the same, and unto grey hairs I will *bear* the burden,—I have made and I will carry, Yes I will *bear* the burden and will deliver. (Is 46:4 Rotherham)

- They carry him about on the shoulder. They *bear* the burden of him—and set him in his place that he may stand,—Out of his place will he not move, —Though one even make outcry unto him he will not answer, Out of one's trouble he will not save him. (Is 46:7 Rotherham)

Thus, he bore and carried away our diseases the very same way he did our sins. But while the lexical definitions of these verbs gave us insight into Isaiah's revelation of the crucifixion, the Day of Atonement which is the superlative type of Jesus' redemptive work, yields an even clearer sense of their meaning.

The Day of Atonement—Shadow of Redemption

Before the resurrection, man had no way to approach God (1 Cor 15:37). God forced his despoiled soul out of the garden and he remained a child of wrath, without God, without hope, until a redeemer could change his nature. Until then, God set up an elaborate sacrificial system. The system couldn't change his nature, but it could cover his sins until the redeemer could come. The system included the Day of Atonement where just once every year the high priest presented offerings to atone for the peoples' sins (*see* Heb 9:7).

On the Day (as they called it), the high priest would wear a white linen robe donned just for the Day's service. Attendant priests would bring in a young bull for the high priest's sin and place it between the temple's porch and the altar. The high priest would face all the people gathered round the temple, lay both hands on the bull, and say:

> YHWH, I have committed iniquity. I have transgressed. I have sinned, me and my house. YHWH, I entreat thee, cover over the iniquities, the transgressions, and the sins which I have committed, transgressed, and sinned before you, me and my house, even as it is written in the law

of Moses, your servant: "For, on that day will He cover over for you to make you clean; from all your transgressions. Before YHWH you will be cleansed!"

Every time that he said, "YHWH," those close by would prostrate themselves on the ground while the rest cried out: "Blessed be the Name! The glory of his kingdom is forever!"

After this, the priests would bring forth two goats, both symbolizing sin. They were supposed to look alike in size and value because they were symbolically just one sacrifice. Traditionally, the Jews were so earnest to carry out this intent that they even tried to arrange it so the goats could be bought at the same time from the same dealer.

They were brought and placed, facing the temple. The high priest would stand between them, facing the people. The priests would bring an urn to him and he'd draw lots. For one, he'd draw *al YHWH*. For the other, *al 'Azazel*. He'd tie a tongue-shaped piece of red cloth around *al YHWH's* throat and another one to *al 'Azazel's* horn. Then he'd turn *al 'Azazel* around to face the people.

He'd move over to the bull, put his hands on it again, confess his sins again, and then slit its throat. He'd pool its blood into a bowl, and give it to one of his attendants. Then he'd arrange some frankincense into a dish and take it with a coal-burning censer into the Holy of Holies.

The Holy of Holies was a cordoned area in the back of the temple. A veil, four inches thick, acted as its door. Behind the veil sat the ark of the covenant—a gold inlaid box containing Moses' tablets, Aaron's staff, and a golden pot filled with manna in it. Two gold cherubim angels stood on the top of either side. Atop the ark, in the middle of the cherubim's wings, was YHWH's presence, the shekinah glory.

When the high priest ducked behind the veil, there was no visible light except his small censer and YHWH's glowing shekinah's presence on the Mercy Seat. He'd stand before the Mercy Seat and carefully empty the frankincense into his hand and throw it on his censer. Then he'd wait. Once the incense's smoke filled the room, he'd retrace his steps—backwards—muttering a prayer.

After this incense offering, he'd enter the Holy of Holies again, but this time with the bull's blood. He'd stand again in front of the Mercy Seat, dip his finger in the bowl of blood, and then sprinkle it—once up and seven times down—counting as he did so. He'd retrace his steps as before and lay the bowl in front of the veil.

Then he'd come to the goat, *al YHWH*, lay his hands on it, and confess the people's sin over it (Lv 4:24). He'd slit its throat and sprinkle its blood on the Mercy Seat the same way he did the bull's. He'd then take both the goat's blood and the bull's and sprinkle them on the veil and then on the horns of the altar.

Then he went to *al 'Azazel*, which was still facing the people.

He'd lay his hands on its head, saying:

YHWH, they have committed iniquity; they have transgressed; they have sinned. Your people, the house of Israel. YHWH cover over, I ask you, their iniquities, their transgressions, and their sins, which they have wickedly committed, transgressed, and sinned before you. Thy people, the house of Israel. As it stands written in the law of Moses, your servant, saying: "For on that day shall it be covered for you to make you clean from all your sins before YHWH. You will be cleansed!"

And, as the multitude would lay prostrate, he'd say over them: "You shall be cleansed!" Then al 'Azazel, burdened with the people's sin, would be led out by a strong man, a non-Israelite, through Solomon's Porch and the eastern gate. He'd abandon the goat in the desert, leaving it to die there.

The goats, a shadow, show the depth of Isaiah's *carried* and *bore*. When the high priest laid his hands on the goats' heads (the two representing one sacrifice and one type) and confessed their sins, the Israelites didn't think of them as mere symbols. The Hebrew is more pungent than that. It called offerings *sin* or *guilt*—the animal bore the name for which it was sacrificed. So, when the high priest confessed the people's sins over *al YHWH*, the Israelites thought, "There goes my sin." This was also true with *al 'Azazel*: "so shall the goat bear upon him all their iniquities into a lone land" (Lv 16:22). When the strong man led him out, the people literally saw their sin carried away from them.

The Believer's Grounds for Healing

The high priest did in type what God did in reality. He filled Jesus to the full with the sins of us all. He made him sin—cursed and forsaken. Jesus felt its full weight: "My God, my God, why have you forsaken me? Why are you so far away? So far from the words of my roaring? My God! I cry in the day and you don't hear me. At night and I've no rest. I'm a worm and not a man" (Ps 22:1-2). The sin so marred him that he didn't even look like a man anymore (Is 52:14).

Crushed with sin and sickness, he became a man bearing our pains: "I am poured out like water, and all my bones are out of joint. My heart? It's like wax melted in the midst of my bowels. My strength is dried up like an old pot. My tongue cleaves to my gums. You've brought me down to the dust of death" (Ps 22:14-15). On the cross, he died the death of *al YHWH*.

But that wasn't the end of it. Like *al 'Azazel*, he carried sin and sickness away from us to a lone land— the heart of the earth—yielding himself to the pangs of spiritual death for three days and nights (Acts 2:24). God was pleased to crush him, bruise him this way because it paved the way for our healing—*by his bruise there is healing for us.*

The believer's ground for healing doesn't lie in good works, ornamental prayers, or even desperate need: it lies in the Righteous One, who humbly and sacrificially suffered the tortures of the damned for him.

9

The Apostles

Matthew – He Bore Our Sicknesses

Matthew, an apostle and witness to the crucifixion, tethered Isaiah's revelation to physical healing. One night, people brought the sick and demon-possessed for Jesus to heal (Mt 8:16). Matthew wrote that Jesus cast out the spirits with his word and healed all the sick so that Isaiah's *Himself, our sicknesses he took and our diseases bore* might be fulfilled (Mt 8:17). The context where he invoked Isaiah not only shows its application to physical healing, but his vocabulary does, too. He used *astheneias* for sicknesses and *nosous* for diseases, words used throughout the new testament to refer to physical disease:

- Now when the sun was setting, all they that had any sick (*asthenoutas* – ἀσθενοῦτας) with divers diseases (*nosois* – νόσοις) brought them unto him; and he laid his hands on every one of them, and healed them. (Lk 4:40)

- But so much the more went there a fame abroad of him: and great multitudes came together to hear, and to be healed by him of their infirmities (*astheneiōn* – ἀσθενειῶν). (Lk 5:15)

- And a certain woman, which had been healed of evil spirits and infirmities (*astheneiōn* – ἀσθενειῶν), Mary called Magdalene, out of whom went seven devils. (Lk 8:2)

- And, behold, there was a woman which had a spirit of infirmity (*asthenias* – ἀσθενείας) eighteen years, and was bowed together, and could in no wise lift herself up. (Lk 13:11)

- And he healed many that were sick of divers diseases (*nosois* – νόσοις), and cast out many devils; and suffered not the devils to speak, because they knew him. (Mk 1:34)

- So that from his body were brought unto the sick handkerchiefs or aprons, and the diseases (*nosous* – νόσους) departed from them, and the evil spirits went out of them. (Acts 19:12)

Some say that Isaiah's passage only applies to sin. They point out that the Septuagint (a Greek translation of the Masoretic text finished 300 to 100 years before Jesus was born) had substituted *sins* for Isaiah's *sicknesses:*

Οὗτος τὰς ἁμαρτίας ἡμῶν φέρει, καὶ περὶ ἡμῶν
ὀδυνᾶται
He bears our sins, and is pained for us

They also point out that Matthew relied on the
Septuagint for old testament quotes like those in
Matthew 21:16 and 21:42. There, he quoted the
Septuagint exactly.

But Matthew didn't follow the Septuagint with
Himself our sicknesses he took and our diseases bore.
Instead, he penned his own Greek translation that
preserved Isaiah's original *sicknesses* and *diseases*. God
apparently inspired him to ignore the Septuagint's sins
to preserve the truth of Jesus' sickness-bearing.

Just a Messianic Claim?

Some say that Matthew's verse only speaks of Jesus'
claim of divinity: "It stands as an evidence and proof of
Christ's Messianic claim." Proof that he was God's son. If
that were so, then no new testament believer would have
grounds to believe that Jesus bore his sickness.

At first glance, the claim sounds plausible. But a
closer look shows that it couldn't be so; it flouts *Sola
Scriptura*—the doctrine that God can't contradict
himself in scripture. If, by healing all those people that
night Jesus was proving himself to be God's son, then he
should have been able to go anywhere he wanted to cast
out devils and heal the sick. But he didn't. In Nazareth,
he couldn't do much of anything except heal a few

minor illnesses (Mk 6:5). So, if Matthew had written *Himself bore our sicknesses and carried our diseases* as a messianic claim, then we'd understand that there are diseases and oppressions that God, himself, can't heal.

Saying that it was a messianic claim also ignores the meaning of *ours.* Matthew quoted one line out of Isaiah's prophecy. The whole passage reads:

> Despised was he and forsaken of men,
> Man of pains, and familiar with sickness,—
> Yea like one from whom the face is hidden
> Despised, and we esteemed him not.
>
> Yet surely our sicknesses he carried,
> And, as for our pains, he bore the burden of them,—
> But we accounted him stricken
> Smitten of God, and degraded.
>
> Yet he was pierced for transgressions that were ours,
> Was crushed for iniquities that were ours,—
> The chastisement for our well-being was upon him,
> And by his bruise there is healing for us.

The *our* used for sicknesses and pains is the same *our* used for transgressions and iniquities. Since o*ur transgressions* and *our iniquities* doesn't just apply to those healed under Jesus' earthly ministry but to all believers, *our sicknesses* and *our pains* must apply to all believers too. No one could say that *he was despised . . . pierced for transgressions that were ours* applies to all believers, but everything in between those phrases just pertain to Jesus' earthly ministry.

Matthew also used ἡμῶν, the ordinary Greek word for *our*. Peter, Paul, and John used it too, for all believers:

- For I delivered unto you first of all that which also I received: that Christ died for *our* sins according to the scriptures. (1 Co 15:3 ASV)

- who his own self bare *our* sins in his body upon the tree, that we, having died unto sins, might live unto righteousness; by whose stripes ye were healed. (1 Pt 2:24 ASV)

- Herein is love, not that we loved God, but that he loved us, and sent his Son to be the expiation for *our* sins. (1 Jn 4:10 RSV)

If he was just referring to those healed under Jesus' earthly ministry, he would have used ὑμῶν, Greek for *their* or *of them*—Himself, their sicknesses he took and the diseases of them he bore. But he didn't, which means that it applies to all believers, not just those healed under Jesus' earthly ministry.

That It Might Be Fulfilled

Some, still clinging to a messianic claim, point to Matthew's past tense of fulfill —*that it might be fulfilled*:

"He used the past tense which means he was speaking just about those people healed under Jesus' ministry. He hadn't gone to the cross yet, so it couldn't include believers today." Given the way Matthew used the past tense of fulfilled, that logic doesn't hold.

After Jesus healed a man of a withered hand, the Pharisees went outside to plot about how to kill him (Mt 12:12-17). When he caught wind of this, Jesus left. A horde of people followed after him and he healed them all. Matthew wrote that he healed them so that Isaiah's prophecy in Isaiah 42 might be fulfilled (Mt 12:17). Matthew ticked off the prophecy:

- I'll put my Spirit on him.

- He'll show judgment to the Gentiles.

- He won't strive or cry. Neither will any man hear his voice in the streets.

- A bruised reed shall he not break, and a smoking flax he shall not quench;

- Till he send for his judgment to victory;

- And in his name shall the Gentiles trust.
He used the past tense (aorist in the Greek) *that it might be fulfilled* even though at least three parts hadn't yet happened: in his name shall the Gentiles trust, judgment to the Gentiles, and his vengeance to victory. These hadn't been fulfilled because Jesus said that he

was only sent to Israel (Mt 15:24); the gospel wasn't open to the Gentiles until his resurrection (*see* Acts 9 – Paul's apostleship to the Gentiles; Acts 10 – Peter's vision of the unclean animals).

So why did he use the aorist (past tense) if the prophecy hadn't yet come to pass? It's a Greek thing. Sometimes a writer would describe an event that hadn't yet happened using the past tense to emphasize the certainty of it happening (Daniel Wallace, *Greek Grammar Beyond the Basics* 563-64; Maximillian Zerwick, *Biblical Greek* 250, 251). Matthew wasn't the only writer who did this. Mark did it for answered prayer (Mk 11:24 – believe that you have *received*); John quoted Jesus using it when Judas went out to betray him (Jn 13:31 – "now the Son of Man is glorified"); and Paul used it to describe the believers' blessed hope of glorification (Rom 8:30 – those he saved, he also glorified).

By saying *that it might be fulfilled*, Matthew merely sought to stress how all healing stems from Jesus' sickness-bearing on the cross. So *Himself took our sicknesses and bare our diseases* should be taken at its plain meaning.

Peter – You Were Healed

Peter also preached that redemption includes physical healing. In his first letter to the church, he reaffirmed the full measure of the Gospel: Who, our sins he bore up in his body on the tree so that we, getting away from our sins, might live in righteousness—by whose bruise you were healed (1 Pt 2:24).

He used *anēnegken* (ἀνήνεγκεν) for *bore up*, *mōlōpi* (μώλωπι) for bruise, and *iomai* (ἰάθητε) for healed. *Anēnegken* is used to describe a priest offering a sacrifice on an altar. Bruise is singular (he tracks Isaiah 53:5 exactly: τῷ μώλωπι αὐτοῦ (*to mōlōpi autou*)). In the Greek, it's a dative of instrument: the means by which something is accomplished. And *iomai* means physical healing. By using these words, Peter reiterates how Jesus' becoming sin paved the way for the believer's healing: Who, without any sin, offered himself—his body—up on a cross, like a priest would offer a sacrifice on an altar, and he took within himself (Isaiah: God laid upon him) our sins and by this bruise, you are healed.

Some argue that *ye were healed* speaks only of salvation because it's nestled in the context of Jesus taking on sin and the believer's righteousness.

While it does speak of salvation (Jesus' sacrifice on the cross is the means of our salvation), it also speaks to physical healing. Every time *iomai* is used in the new testament, it's associated with physical healing:

- The centurion answered and said, Lord, I am not worthy that thou shouldest come under my roof: but speak the word only, and my servant shall be healed (*iathesetai* – ἰαθήσεται).(Mt 8:8)

- And Jesus said unto the centurion, Go thy way; and as thou hast believed, so be it done unto thee.

And his servant was healed (*iathe* – ἰάθη) in the selfsame hour. (Mt 8:13)

- For this people's heart is waxed gross, and their ears dull of hearing, and their eyes they have closed; lest at any time they should see with their eyes and hear with their ears, and should understand with their heart, and should be converted, and I should heal (*iasomai* – ἰασομαι) them. (Mt 13:15)

- Then Jesus answered and said unto her, O woman, great is thy faith: be it unto thee even as thou wilt. And her daughter was made whole (*iathe* – ἰάθη) from that very hour. (Mt 15:28)

- The Spirit of the Lord is upon me, because he hath anointed me to preach the gospel to the poor; he hath sent me to heal (*iasasthai* – ἰάσασθαι) the brokenhearted, to preach deliverance to the captives, and recovering of sight to the blind, to set at liberty them that are bruised. (Lk 4:18) (Textus Receptus)

- And straightway the fountain of her blood was dried up; and she felt in her body that she was healed (*iatai* – ἴαται) of that plague. (Mk 5:29)

- And it came to pass on a certain day, as he was teaching that there were Pharisees and doctors of the law sitting by, which were come out of every town of Galilee, and Judaea, and Jerusalem: and the power of the Lord was present to heal (*iasthai* – ἰᾶσθαι) them. (Lk 5:17)

- And he came down with them, and stood in the plain, and the company of his disciples, and a great multitude of people out of all Judaea and Jerusalem, and from the sea coast of Tyre and Sidon, which came to hear him, and to be healed (*iathenai* – ἰαθῆναι) of their diseases; (Lk 6:17)

- And the whole multitude sought to touch him: for there went virtue out of him, and healed (*iato* – ἰᾶτο) them all. (Lk 6:19)

- Wherefore neither thought I myself worthy to come unto thee: but say in a word, and my servant shall be healed. (*iathesetai* – ἰαθήσεται) (Lk 7:7)

- And when the woman saw that she was not hid, she came trembling, and falling down before him, she declared unto him before all the people for what cause she had touched him, and how she was healed (*iathe* – ἰάθη) immediately. (Lk 8:47)

- And he sent them to preach the kingdom of God, and to heal (*iasthai* – ἰᾶσθαι) the sick. (Lk 9:2)

- And as he was yet a coming, the devil threw him down, and tare him. And Jesus rebuked the unclean spirit, and healed (*iasato* – ἰάσατο) the child, and delivered him again to his father. (Lk 9:42)

- And they held their peace. And he took him, and healed (*iasato* – ἰάσατο) him, and let him. go; (Lk 14:4)

- And one of them, when he saw that he was healed (*iathe* – ἰάθη), turned back, and with a loud voice glorified God. (Lk 17:15)

- And Jesus answered and said, Suffer ye thus far. And he touched his ear, and healed (*iasato* – ἰάσατο) him. (Lk 22:51)

- When he heard that Jesus was come out of Judea into Galilee, he went unto him, and besought him that he would come down, and heal (*iasetai* – ἰάσηται) his son: for he was at the point of death. (Jn 4:47)

- And he that was healed (*iatheis* – ἰαθεὶς) wist not who it was: Jesus had conveyed himself away, a multitude being in that place. (Jn 5:13)

- He hath blinded their eyes, and hardened their heart; that they should not see with their eyes, nor understand with their heart, and be converted, and I should heal (*iasomai* – ἰάσωμαι) them. (Jn 12:40)

- And as the lame man which was healed (*iathentos* – ἰαθέντος) held Peter and John, all the people ran together unto them in the porch that is called Solomon's, greatly wondering .(Acts 3:11)

- For the man was above forty years, on whom this miracle of healing (*iaseos* – ἰάσεως) shewed. (Acts 4:22)

- By stretching forth thine hand to heal (*iasin* – ἴασιν); and that signs and wonders may be done by the name of thy holy child Jesus. (Acts 4:30)

- And Peter said unto him, Aeneas, Jesus Christ maketh thee whole (*iatai* – ἰᾶταί): arise, and take thy bed. And he arose immediately.   (Acts 9:34)

- How God anointed Jesus of Nazareth with the Holy Ghost and with power: who went about doing good, and healing (*iōmenos* – ἰώμενος) all that were oppressed of the devil; for God was with him. (Acts 10:38)

- And it came to pass, that the father of Publius lay sick of a fever and of a bloody flux: to whom Paul entered in, and prayed, and laid his hands on him, and healed (*iasato* – ἰάσατο) him. (Acts 28:8)

- For the heart of this people is waxed gross, and their ears dull of hearing, and their eyes have they closed; lest they should see with their eyes, and hear with their ears, and understand with their heart, and should be converted, and I should heal (*iasomai* – ἰάσωμαι) them. (Acts 28:27)

- And God hath set some in the church, first apostles, secondarily prophets, thirdly teachers, after that miracles, then gifts of healings (*iamaton* – ἰαμάτων), helps, governments, diversities of tongues. (1 Cor 12:28)

- Have all gifts of healings (*iamaton* – ἰαμάτων)? do all speak with tongues? do all interpret? (1 Cor 12:30)

- And straight paths make for your feet, that that which is lame may not be turned aside, but rather be healed (*iathe* – ἰάθη). (Heb 12:13)

- Confess your faults to one another, and pray one for another, that ye may be healed (*iathete* – ἰαθῆτε). The effectual prayer of a righteous man availeth much. (Jas 5:16)

If Peter hadn't meant physical healing, he would have written: by his bruise you were born-again. He was certainly familiar with the term (*see* 1 Pt 1:23 – born-again (ἀναγεγεννημένοι) of incorruptible seed).

Why did he use the past tense (*you were healed*)? To emphasize that the work has been finished. Jesus only had to die once to provide for our healing; he doesn't have to die again (Rom 6:10 – he died unto sin once).

- For when we were yet without strength, in due time Christ died (ἀπέθανε, *apethane*, second aorist) for the ungodly. (Rom 5:6)

- For I delivered unto you first of all that which I also received, how that Christ died (*apethanen*, ἀπέθανεν, second aorist) for our sins according to the scriptures. (1 Cor 15:3)

- And they sung a new song, saying, Thou art worthy to take the book, and to open the seals thereof: for thou wast slain, and hast redeemed (*ēgorasas*, ἠγόρασας, aorist) us to God by thy blood out of every kindred, and tongue, and people, and nation; (Rv 5:9)

God's provision for healing is an accomplished fact. The believer doesn't need to add anything to Jesus' work; he only needs to appropriate *by his bruise you were healed.*

Paul – He Became a Curse

Paul is another witness who ties healing to redemption, and he received his revelation directly from the Lord (Gal 1:12 – neither received of man, nor taught it, but by revelation of Jesus Christ).

In Deuteronomy, the Lord gave instructions to the Israelites just before they were going to cross over into the promised land. First, he told them that they'd be blessed if they hearkened to his voice and did all that he commanded them to do. His blessings included health and healing: Blessed shall be the fruit of your body and the fruit of your lands (Dt 28:1-14).

But with the blessings came warnings of a curse. The Lord said that if they did not obey his commands, they'd suffer every curse (*katarai* – κατάραι) of the law. And the curses included every kind of sickness and disease, from madness and blindness, to tuberculosis, scabs, boils, fevers, and blotches (Dt 28:15, 21, 22, 27, 28). All without a chance of healing (Dt 28:27).

Paul was familiar with the word *katarai*, Greek for curses. He relied heavily on the Septuagint, the Greek translation of the Hebrew Masoretic texts, for his old testament references (Romans alone has over 30 direct quotations from the Septuagint, and he also quoted from it in his letters to the Corinthians and Galatians).

He understood Isaiah's *he laid on him the sins of us all.* He wrote in Corinthians *God made him to be sin* so that we could be redeemed. In Galatians, he said it another way: Christ, being made a curse for us, redeemed us from the curse of the law (Gal 3:13). Paul used the very same word, *kataras*, found in the Septuagint's Deuteronomy. What was the curse of the law? In part, the sicknesses and diseases that fell to all who disobeyed the Lord. By Jesus innocently bearing sin and becoming a curse for us, Paul says, we're relieved from having to bear the diseases that the law brought on all who broke it.

Acts demonstrates that this is what Paul preached. In Lystra, it says that he preached the gospel and Paul perceived that one in his audience, a man who had been crippled from birth, possessed the faith to be healed (Acts 14:8-10). Paul commanded him to stand upright, and the man was healed instantly. If Paul hadn't preached that Jesus redeemed us from sickness and disease, how could the man have had faith to be healed?

He preached the same truth to the Corinthians. Many in the church were sickly and some had even died prematurely (1 Cor 11:30). He recounted the Lord's supper: Jesus said of his body, "Take, eat, this is my body, the one on your behalf," and his blood, "This cup is the new testament in my blood." And told them, "For as often as you eat this bread and drink the cup, you proclaim the Lord's death until he comes." He said that they had become sick and some had died because they didn't rightly discern the Lord's body. They didn't esteem his becoming a curse and carrying their sicknesses for them. Because of that, Satan was able to assume the advantage (*see* Acts 10:38 – disease is Satanic oppression).

10

Seated With Christ

All things are cleansed with blood. Without blood-shedding, there's no remission of sins (Heb 9:22). This was the truth behind the Day of Atonement. The high priest could not just appear before the Mercy Seat empty-handed and ask for the people's forgiveness. He had to have blood. A goat not only had to be offered—its throat slit and its blood pooled in a bowl—its blood had to be ceremoniously applied for the people's sins to be covered. Jesus had to do the same thing with his own blood to procure our redemption from Satan's authority (Heb 9:24).

Christ is Exalted

It was his utter reliance on God—the yielding of the Righteous One to death—that paved the way for healing. He had to be crucified through weakness (2 Cor 13:4) and yield himself to the lordship of death (Rom 6:9). In becoming sin for us, Jesus had to wholly rely on God to vindicate him. After suffering the tortures of a sin-ladened man for three days and nights in Hades (Mt 12:40), God raised him up when every man could become born-again and healed (Rom 4:25).

On the third day, God thundered, "Thy throne, O God, is for ever and ever! A scepter of righteousness is the scepter of your kingdom!" down into the depths of Hades, and Jesus was made alive. In that, God disarmed the demonic powers and made them a public mockery (Col 2:15); the pangs of death couldn't hold Jesus anymore (Acts 2:24). Once he resurrected Jesus with new life, he appointed him high priest of the new covenant (Heb 5:5). A covenant that Jesus would ratify and remit our sins by his own blood (Acts 20:28).

Mary met Jesus at the tomb that day. When she arrived, she saw a man wearing all white and thought he was the gardener (gardeners wore white work clothes then). He wasn't. He responded, "Mary," and Mary saw that he was Jesus. He was wearing all white because he hadn't finished his priestly role. By his own sacrifice on the cross and the three days, he had fulfilled the types of al 'Azazel and al YHWH, but he still had to present the blood before the Mercy Seat. Hearing her name, she sought to hug him. But he said, "Don't touch me. I'm ascending to my Father, and your Father, and my God, and your God." He was ceremoniously clean (Heb 10:20) and was taking his blood to the holy place in heaven.

He did ascend and presented his blood before the Father, obtaining an eternal salvation for us (Heb 9:12). His sacrifice not only remitted our sin, it purged our consciences—renewing them with his own renewed life.

Once he had accomplished this, God bestowed on him the name above every name (Phil 2:9) and seated him at his own right hand (Heb 1:3).

Exalted With Him

Jesus qualified as an acceptable sacrifice because he was the first man to ever wholly cast himself on God (*see* Mt 27:43; 1 Tm 3:16). Through his utter reliance on the Father—the yielding of the Righteous One to becoming sin on the cross—God raised him to new life (Jn 8:12). He is the *archegos* of life—the originator and founder of the spirit of Christ who continues as leader and head of the *ekklesia* (Acts 3:15). In the wisdom of God, we've been raised with him and seated with him (Eph 2:6). We are, in fact, partakers of his own divine nature (Rom 8:9 – if any man doesn't possess the spirit of Christ, he is none of his).

Because of his finished work and our identification with him, we aren't defenseless to the demonic oppressions described in Acts 10:38 (healing all those oppressed of the devil). We've been translated out of the authority of darkness (Col 1:13, 14) and are no longer animated by the prince of the power of the air (Eph 2:3). We are in Christ, subject only to the head of the *ekklēsia* and to God.

So we may resist Satan with our authority in Christ and with the power of the spirit (Jas 4:7 – resist the devil, and he will flee from you; 1 Pt 5:8 – resist the devil steadfast in the faith). He may be an accuser

(Zec 3:1), but he has to beg off once we stand in Christ's finished work (Eph. 6:13). The believer doesn't have to fight. He only has to hold over him the victory that he shares with Christ. Satan may try to test his resolve to stand, but he can't withstand the believer's authority once it's been exercised.

The Believer is to Glorify God in His Body

The believer is not redeemed from Satanic oppression in his body, but he's charged to glorify God with it. Paul wrote, "Don't you realize that your body is the temple of God and you're not your own? You were bought with a price. So glorify God in your body and your spirit, which are God's" (1 Cor 6:20, Textus Receptus). *Which* in the Greek is the nominative plural *hatina* (ἅτινά). Being plural, it modifies both spirit and body; the purchase price of redemption didn't just cover the believer's inner man, but his body too (*see* Rv 5:9; 2 Pt 2:1). Thus the believer is not only freed from sin, he's charged to not let sin reign in his body or yield to unrighteousness (Rom 6:12-13). A satanically oppressed body, one given to disease, doesn't discharge that imperative.

Spiritual Quickening

In combatting disease, the believer not only has his authority in Christ to wield, but also the dynamo of his reborn spirit. Paul wrote of this power: But if the spirit of him that raised up Jesus from the dead dwells in you, he that raised up Christ from the dead will also make alive your mortal bodies by the means of the spirit that dwells in you (Rom 8:11). The reborn human spirit fuses life into the believer's death-doomed body, animating it to drive out any kind of oppression of the adversary.

Some have said that Paul was speaking in Romans 8:11 of the day when our bodies will be glorified and not the church age. But that wouldn't be right for a number of reasons. First, the context shows that he's writing about believers in the church age. He says that if we have the spirit of Christ—the reborn human spirit—then our bodies are dead because of sin. Then he says that the reborn spirit gives life to the body and follows with saying that we, as believers, aren't debtors to the flesh to live after it. We can mortify the deeds of the body through the work of the spirit. When our bodies are glorified, there won't be any need to mortify the deeds of the body, so he must be speaking of our day and time (*see* Rom 8:13).

Second, when he wrote that the spirit dwells in us, he wrote dwell (*oikei* – οἰκει) in the present tense and contrasted it with mortal bodies (*thnēta somata* – θνητα σωματα) or death-doomed bodies. He used that term in Rom 6:12, saying: Don't let sin reign in your mortal (or death-doomed) body (*see also* 2 Cor 4:11—we are to manifest the life of Christ in these bodies which are subject to death). Glorified bodies aren't death-doomed; they've passed from death unto life. If the believer has the power to overcome sin in his body, he has the power to stand against sin's offspring, disease.

The plain meaning of Rom 8:11 is that the reborn human spirit is a dynamo of life that gives the believer the power to mortify the deeds in the flesh, even when the flesh wants to give in to oppression.

11

The Church's Commission to Heal

Even as Jesus' death, burial, and resurrection exalted the believer to God's own right hand, a place where he could receive and enforce his own healing, Jesus commissioned the church to continue his healing ministry. She has been granted the same distribution of the Holy Ghost, the one without measure, that rested on Jesus when he walked the earth.

The Greater Works

After Judas left the last supper to betray him, Jesus turned to the rest of his disciples and said, "Where I go, you can't come." Peter asked, "Lord, where are you going?" Jesus answered him, "Where I go, you can't follow me now, but you can follow me afterwards." Peter piped up, "Why can't I go? I'll lay my life down for you" (Jn 13:35-36). Jesus then began preparing the disciples for his death and later ascension.

One of the more provocative statements that he made to them was: "I say this to all of you, the one that believes on me, the works that I'm doing? He'll do them. And not only those, but he'll do even greater than these because I'm going to the Father." His ascension would bring about an even greater healing ministry than he had; the distributions of the Holy Ghost and power would not be poured out on a lone individual, but on the whole church.

After he had provided them proofs of his resurrection, showing them his hands and his side, he breathed into them. "Receive holy spirit," he said, and they became born again (Jn 20:22). He told them that all authority had been given to him, then he turned around and delegated it to them, the church (Mt 28:18 – "all authority is given me . . . go therefore"). He commissioned them to cast out devils and heal the sick, like he had done with the twelve and the seventy (Mk 16:18), but he told them to wait until they received the power from on high (Lk 24:49). That power wouldn't come until he ascended to the Father.

Forty days after he was resurrected, he ascended (Lk 1:3). Ten days later the power fell (Acts 2:1). The disciples had all gathered in Jerusalem (where he had instructed them to go) and suddenly the sound of a windstorm came out of heaven. The sound filled the house where they were staying, and tongues of fire appeared over each one of their heads. They were all filled with the power and began speaking in other tongues (Acts 2:4). Peter and the others began declaring how God had resurrected Jesus and made him the *archēgos* (Prince, Captain) of the new life (Acts 3:15). And God began confirming his word with accompanying signs (Mk 16:20; Heb 2:4).

The Church Continues Jesus' Ministry

The first healing recorded after the anointing was poured out was the man at the Gate Beautiful (Acts 3:1-8). Peter and John, going up together to the temple at the time of prayer, saw a lame man—lame since birth —asking for alms by the temple's gate. Jesus evidently hadn't healed him (*see* Mt 24:1; Mk 11:11; Jn 7:14; Jn 10:23 – Jesus had taught in and around the temple).

On this particular day, the gifts of the Spirit manifested. Like Jesus and the man at the pool of Bethesda, Peter didn't preach to the beggar for faith to come, but he acted on the presence of the gifts of healing. He said, "I don't have any silver or gold, but what I do have, I give you: In the name of Jesus Christ of Nazareth rise up and walk!" He took the man by the hand, lifted him up, and the man was healed instantly.

Peter and John took him in to the temple where a crowd gathered because everyone knew who the man was. Peter responded to them, "Why are you looking at us like we made this man walk by our own power or holiness? The God of Abraham, Isaac, Jacob, the God of our fathers, he has glorified his Son Jesus whom you delivered up, and denied before Pilate, when he thought he'd let him go. You denied the Holy One and the Just, and wanted a murderer to be granted to you. You killed the Prince of life and God's raised him up from the dead. We're witnesses. And his name—through faith in his name—has made this man, whom you see and know, strong. The faith that's by him [Jesus] has given him this perfect wholeness before all of you."

Speaking of "his name—through faith in his name," Peter confirmed Jesus' directive that they, the church, would lay hands on the sick and the sick would be healed. Here, fulfillment came through the operation of the Spirit which gave Peter a platform to preach the Gospel to Jews in the temple. Five thousand were saved that day even though the priests and the Sadducees tried to stop them by throwing Peter and John in prison (Acts 4:1-4).

When Peter and John were eventually released, they made their way back to the company of disciples. Then they all lifted up their voices in one accord, asking God to continue to heal: "And now, Lord, behold their threatenings: and grant unto us that we may speak your word with all boldness, by stretching forth your hand to heal. And that signs and wonders may be done by the name of your holy child Jesus."

This prayer didn't involve some mystical inner healing. They prayed for physical healing. The Sadducees had told Peter and John not to teach or preach in Jesus' name strictly because of the lame man's healing (Acts 4:16-18). The disciples' prayer was a direct response to the Sadducees' efforts to quash the miraculous gospel. They asked God to stretch forth his hand to heal (εἰς ἴασιν)—the very same word (ἴασιν) used for physical healing throughout the new testament (*see* 1 Pt 2:24 above). And that wasn't all. They also asked for signs and wonders—miraculous workings in the natural realm—by the means of Jesus' name. They had no doubt that they numbered among the believing ones that Jesus spoke of before his crucifixion; healings and signs were to going to accompany them wherever they preached the gospel.

The Healing Anointing Continues

The primary way that Jesus ministered to the sick was through a tangible healing anointing. Pentecost's power from on high is a continuation of that anointing, distributed among different individuals in varying strengths.

Paul was specifically called to preach the Gospel to the heathen. During his ministry, he'd support himself through making leather crafts when donations were down (Acts 18:3; 1 Cor 4:11-12). In making tents and other goods, he wore aprons and used work cloths. Like Elisha's staff, his aprons and cloths would become infused with the tangible anointing that rested on him (*see* Lk 6:19). People, in fact, took them and laid them on the sick and demon-possessed. The anointing in them healed the sick and drove the demons out of those possessed (Acts 19:11-12).

When he landed on Melita, Paul learned that the island's chief, Publius, was sick with a fever and bloody flux. He went to him and laid his hands on him. The anointing healed Publius and Paul was able to heal on the island others who had diseases (Acts 28:6-9).

The healing anointing apparently rested more strongly on Peter than it did Paul. When people learned that Peter would be visiting, they brought the sick into the streets and laid them on all kinds of couches and beds, hoping that at least his shadow would fall on some of them (Acts 5:15). His healing anointing was so strong that they thought if they just got close enough, they'd be healed. And the people who did this were "healed every one" (Acts 5:16).

Peter and Paul both saw this tangible anointing as an extension of Jesus' own ministry. When Peter arrived at Aenaeas's house, he said, "Jesus heals you," present tense (Acts 9:34). And Paul, writing to the Romans, said, "For I won't dare to speak of any of those things that Christ hasn't done by me, to make the Gentiles obedient, by word and deed, through mighty signs and wonders, by the power of the spirit of God" (Rom 15:18).

There are those who say that the church's anointing expired with the last of the apostles; the anointing was given just to validate new testament scripture. But there isn't any authority for that. Paul said that tongues, which came and was made possible by the enduement of power from on high, would cease when that which is perfect—the manifestation of the sons of God—is come (1 Cor 13:8-10). Acts isn't just a historical record; the Lord has intended to confirm His Word with accompanying signs throughout the balance of the church age (see Heb 2:4).

12

The Need for Faith

The only currency that counts with God is faith—the believed report of what he's said and what he's done. Nothing else procures his benefits. Nothing.

The Mix of Faith

The Israelites made it to the border of Canaan—the land God had promised to Abraham and his seed—and the Lord told Moses to send out one man from each of the twelve tribes to search it out. Moses chose his twelve to bring back a report about the land and the people living in it. And, since it was grape season, he told them to bring some grapes back, too, for a look.

The twelve explored the land for forty days. During their trip they cut down grapes to bring back. The grapes were so big that they had to string them between two men on a pole. They also picked up some pomegranates and figs.

When they got back to camp, they raised the grapes before the people, saying, "Yes, the land, indeed, is a land flowing with milk and honey," just as God had promised to Abraham (Gn 17:8; Ex 3:8). And then they added, "But there are giants in the land. And the cities have huge walls. And we saw the sons of Anak (giants) there."

Giants? Huge Walls? That created quite a stir though Caleb, one of the twelve, sought to reassure them: Let's go possess for we are sure to prevail!" But the other spies stood up and argued against him: "We can't go up against these people; they're much stronger than we are." And that set off murmuring through the people that the promised land was a land that eats its own and everyone who lived there were giants. They'd be as helpless as grasshoppers, they thought.

"Oh! that we had died in Egypt! Or even here in the desert! Yahweh is bringing us to a land to have us killed by the sword! Let's appoint a captain to take us back to Egypt."

Caleb, again—this time with Joshua—aimed to strengthen their faith: "As for the land that we spied out, it's really good. And if Yahweh delights in us, he'll bring us into this land and give it to us. Don't rebel against Yahweh and don't fear the people there. Why, they're our food, for Yahweh is with us."

The Israelites not only didn't listen, they picked up rocks to stone the two. And then the glory of God appeared. God spoke to Moses out of the glory: "How long will these people provoke me? How long before they will believe me?"

And in his anger for their unbelief he swore: "None of those who have seen my glory and the signs that I did in

Egypt, and in the desert, and have put me to proof these ten times, and have not hearkened to my voice shall see the land. None of my despisers shall see it. Their carcasses will fall in the desert and their children will wander for forty years!" (Nm 14:10-11, 22-23).

They were God's chosen people. He had delivered them out of Egypt through ten miraculous plagues, had taken them through the walls of water of the Red Sea, and had shown them his glory in the desert. Yet they didn't enter into the promised land—the land that God had promised to Abraham hundreds of years earlier. Why not? Because of their unbelief (Heb 4:12). They had heard the promise, but they didn't mix it with faith (Heb 4:2 – the word, not being mixed with faith, didn't profit them). They believed the spies' take on the people in the land—"we can't go up against these people"— over what God had said. So, except for Caleb and Joshua, they died in the desert without ever entering into the blessing that God had already provided for them. They that observe lying vanities, the Word says, forsake their own mercy (Ps 31:6; Jon 2:8).

The Eye of Faith

Faith is the conviction of facts unseen—the facts set by the one who calls those things that are not as things that are (Heb 11:1; Rom 4:17). Faith is not a walk out into space; it's a walk on the sure word of prophecy—those facts that God has founded in the unseen realm that are more sure and more solid than the things we see with our natural eyes, which are subject to change.

Abram was ninety-nine years old when the Lord appeared and preached the Gospel to him (Gal 3:8). The Lord said, "I have made you a father of many nations. I will make you tremendously fruitful. Kings will come out from you. So you're no longer Abram, but Abraham (father of a multitude). And I will establish my covenant between me and you and your seed after you. In you, all nations will be blessed" (Gn 17:4-8).

At ninety-nine, Abram was beyond all natural hope of a son (Rom 4:19). And his wife was, too. But those facts didn't deter him; he didn't look to them. He looked only to the promise—the promise of a seed that would bless the nations. He wasn't led to hesitate by unbelief, but waxed strong in faith of the day that his seed would give birth to the redeemer (Jn 8:56 – "Abraham rejoiced to see my day"). God reckoned righteousness to him because his faith wasn't based on anything he saw, but on what God had established as an unseen fact. Unlike the Israelites, he was fully persuaded that what God had promised, he was able to perform (Rom 4:21). And Isaac was born a year later.

After Isaac had grown, God tested Abraham's faith (Gn 22:1-12). "Take Isaac over to the land of Moriah to sacrifice him there on one of the mountains that I tell you to." Abraham didn't hesitate. He rose early the next morning, saddled up his donkeys, and took Isaac and pieces of wood to Moriah. Arriving there, the Lord showed him the mountain. Abraham took Isaac up and laid him on an altar that he had made out of the wood that they had brought. When he raised his knife to slice Isaac's throat, an angel stopped him: "Abraham! Don't lay your hand on your son, for now I know that you revere God and would not even withhold your son from me."

How could Abraham think of sacrificing Isaac, the miraculous son born of a hundred-year-old man and ninety-year-old woman? He could because he was looking solely to the promise: through your seed all nations will be blessed. He knew that Isaac was the channel for the seed of the coming redeemer (Gn 21:12) and that nothing would or could stop the promise from coming to pass, even if he was to sacrifice his son (Heb 11:19 – accounting that God was able to raise him from the dead).

Noah's faith was the same. It had never rained before God visited him (*see* Gn 2:6) and announced his intention to wipe man off the face of the earth, except for Noah and his family (Heb 11:7 – having received intimations of things not seen). God told him to build an ark and, on that word alone, Noah set out to build an ark that could house two (and some seven) of every kind of animal. It took him fifty years or more to finish it, all without a single drop of rain. But he was fully persuaded of the fact of a coming flood without anything more than God's word; it saved him and his family.

Moses, when he had grown up in years, refused to be called the son of Pharoah's daughter. He consciously chose to suffer with the Jews because he believed that the abuse that he suffered for Christ was far better than the wealth of Egypt; his eyes were fixed on the heavenly reward, so he stayed constant (Heb 11:26). The eye of faith doesn't walk by natural sight (2 Cor 5:7). It sees the invisible.

Healing is an Accomplished Fact

Redemption is a finished work, an accomplished fact. Jesus doesn't need to die again to save anyone (Rom 6:10). He emptied himself of his glory; was born of a woman; lived under the law; offered himself upon the cross; became sin; and was resurrected by the operation of God. He obtained an eternal salvation for every man, past and future. That narrative doesn't have to be repeated. All an unsaved man has to do is accept it and receive it.

After Paul had established churches in Galatia, he learned that some teachers had come in to the churches and were telling the new Christians that they had to add to their faith; that they had to do more than just believe and act on what Jesus had accomplished. When Paul heard about this, he was livid. He jealously wrote:

> I'm surprised to hear you moving away so soon from the grace of Christ. You stupid Galatians! How could you be so deceived when Jesus crucified was placarded before your very eyes? I want to know this one thing from you: When you received the gift of the [reborn] spirit, was it because you obeyed some commandment, or because you believed the Gospel message? How is it possible that you have been so deceived? You began in the spirit and now you think you

perfect yourselves somehow by adding
something in the flesh? God bestows his spirit
on you, he works miracles among you—does he
do these things because you added something,
or because you believed his message? Know that
just as Abraham believed God and his faith was
set down as righteous, those who rely on faith
(not works) are the real sons of Abraham.

Abraham didn't seek to add anything to God's promise that all nations would be blessed through him. He was fully persuaded by God's word alone. He held fast that confidence, even in the face of circumstances that said that it couldn't come true. Following this, the promise came to pass.

The same is true for healing. Isaiah saw that Jesus not only became our sin, he bore our sicknesses and carried our diseases: *by his bruise we are healed*. Peter, looking back to the crucifixion, also emphasized how this is an accomplished fact by restating Isaiah's text in the past tense: *by his bruise we were healed*. Like salvation, all the oppressed Christian has to do is believe, accept, and receive it. There isn't anything for him to add. It's unbelief if he does.

13
The Faith That Takes

Jesus laid down precisely how to appropriate God's redemptive promises: "All the things, whatever you are asking for and praying for, believe that you've received them, and you'll have them" (Mk 11:24).

The fig tree stands as an object lesson (Mk 11:13-14; Mt 21:18-22). Jesus and his disciples were walking toward Bethany when Jesus turned off the path to eat some figs because he was hungry. When he came up to the fig tree that he had seen from the road, he saw that it didn't have any figs even though it was the season for them. The disciples overheard him say, "Let no man eat of you hereafter forever!" He made his way back to the path, and they all went on to Bethany together.

The next morning, when they came by the tree, they saw that it had dried up—from the roots. Peter pointed this out to Jesus and he said, "If you have faith, you'll not only do what was done to this fig tree, but if you say to this mountain, 'Move! and be thrown into the sea,' it'll be done. And all—as much as you ask in prayer, you will receive" (Mt 21:22; Mk 11:24). The manifestation of the answer is sure to happen if you don't doubt.

Steps to Appropriate Healing

Receive it. Passive agreement is not receipt. The believer can't just assent to Jesus' sickness bearing. He's got to swallow it. Jesus likened the gospel to an expensive pearl or a great treasure that a man would sell everything he had to get. It's not the casual word, but the engrafted word that saves (Jas 1:21). When the woman with the hemorrhage heard about Jesus' message, she wasn't insouciant about it. She didn't take it as some vapid platitude. She recognized it as the God-breathed gospel and gulped it down hard. The revelation impelled her to fight through a mob to get even just one finger on his robe.

There aren't any hard and fast rules for implanting the word, setting your heart on fire. It might take just one message, one recitation of scripture, one *thus saith God.* Or it may take longer meditation, where his spirit can brush the scales off your eyes so you can better see the bright lights of your redemption. Whatever the case, you must be fully convinced of this: Jesus bore *your* sicknesses and carried away *your* diseases.

Pray it. Prayer is your mark of appropriation. It isn't based on your need, your level of desperation, your good works, or even sympathy. When approaching the throne of grace, you should have just one thing in your hand: the revelation of *by his bruise I was healed.* Your prayer marks the moment when God's appropriation of his gospel and power is set against your oppression of disease.

Possess it. You leave the throne knowing what you've asked for—believe you received. You know he's heard you. You know it, not because of any manifestation or even any signs of improvement. You're not moved by those. You know it only because of his promise that you received what you asked for. You know within yourself that the unseen—your healing—will become the seen by the sole reason of his promise. Your confession is sure. It's in your heart and on your lips. (Out of the abundance of the heart, the mouth speaks.)

Sure, during your times of possession you may be buffeted. Satan comes along with his "Yea, hath God said?" to bring you to doubt the veracity of *our sicknesses he bore.* Or he shoots his arrows of affliction or persecution your way. Symptoms become more severe. Loved ones fuel your mind with doubt and unbelief. But they haven't seen what you've seen. Their eyes are on what's sensual, earthly, and devilish. Yours are set on things above. "It stands written!" you say, instead of stumbling off the rock of the Word. Your battle is not to fight feelings, friends, manifestations, or emasculated doctrine, but only to stand firm on what God has said, what he's already answered (Eph 6:13, 14 – having done all to stand, stand therefore). So, you remain unmoved.

See it. As Jesus promised, faith does become sight. When Daniel discovered that the Israelites had been in captivity for a longer time than what had been prophesied, he set himself to pray (Dn 10:1-14). When the answer didn't immediately manifest, he began a fast. Twenty-one days after he had set himself to pray, an angel appeared to him, saying, "From the first day that you set your heart to understand, your words were heard and I've come for your words. But the Prince of Persia fought me for twenty-one days." God had dispatched the answer right when Daniel had first prayed. The answer —the angel's appearance—manifested well after God had answered Daniel's petition.

You have your answer—not when it manifests—but when you pray. It's a walk of faith, not sight; you're fully persuaded that the answer cannot not come to pass despite all natural evidence to the contrary. But you're not moved by your natural eye. You've set your sights higher, where Jesus sits at God's right hand (Col 3:2). This is your boldness in him: if you ask anything according to what he's provided you in Christ, you know that you have it the moment you asked him for it (1 Jn 5:14-15).

Those healed under Jesus' ministry—blind Bartamaeus, the woman with the issue of blood, the ten lepers and all the others—didn't live under any special dispensation. They didn't enjoy any greater rights or privileges than any born again child of God. When Jesus offered himself on the cross, he bore our sicknesses, and by his resurrection he destroyed the power of the enemy. Healing is the God-given right of every believer. And, like salvation, it's there for the taking.

Questions About Healing

Question:

How can I know that it's God's will to heal me?

The question of God's will about healing was settled in Jesus' death, burial, and resurrection. On the cross, Jesus bore our sicknesses and carried away our diseases. That is an unchangeable, redemptive fact that God, himself, cannot change. Thus, healing is the redemptive privilege of every believer.

Question:

If healing was provided in redemption, why isn't every believer healed?

Healing, like all the benefits we receive from God, depends on faith. Jesus bore the sins of the whole world and yet not everyone is saved. While he has done all to save, some—even most—men will die in their sins because they didn't believe the message and call on his name. Similarly, even though he bore our sicknesses, the believer must accept and receive that fact by faith to receive the benefit of healing.

Question:

My pastor teaches that God is sovereign and he's the one who determines who is sick.

The line of preaching that teaches that God instigates everything from lymphoma to aneurysms to head colds is a pernicious teaching directly contrary to the revelation of scripture (*see* Acts 10:38 – disease is a form of satanic oppression). If God were the author of disease, no believer could pray in faith for healing: it'd be against the revealed will of God. Jesus never refused to heal anyone because God had laid sickness on him. God anointed him to break the yoke of sickness. That pastor's doctrine is just a sophisticated excuse for unbelief.

Question:

My sister looked to be in faith when she prayed to be healed, so why wasn't she?

Though faith has its expressions in acts and in confessions, it is a product of the heart. And as men who look upon outward appearances, sometimes what looks to be faith is not. God is the sole judge of who is in faith.

When Jesus walked down from the mount of transfiguration, he ran into a crowd surrounding his disciples. "What are you disputing with them?" he asked. A man stepped out and said, "My son has a dumb spirit who thrashes him around. I asked your disciples to cast him out, but they couldn't." The disciples had apparently tried to command the spirit to leave the boy (Jesus had given them power to cast out devils – Mt 10:1), but it didn't come out and that riled up a crowd.

After Jesus cast the spirit out, the disciples took him aside and asked, "Why couldn't we cast it out?" Jesus told them flatly it was because of their unbelief (Mt

17:20). Evidently, while they appeared to the crowd to be acting in faith, they weren't.

Jesus said, "All things are possible to the one believing."

Question:

If healing and the laying on of hands is for today, then why don't you just clean out all the hospitals?

Jesus, himself, wasn't able to heal everyone (*see* Mt 13:58). In Mark 5, he visited his hometown of Nazareth and they were offended at him. The Word says that he couldn't do any mighty works in the town except lay his hands on a few sick with minor ailments because of their unbelief (Mk 6:5).

Except for those isolated instances where the gifts of the Spirit are manifest, healing requires faith. In the account of the men who ripped off the roof to have their friend healed, it says that Jesus saw *their* faith. By the way he reported it—Jesus, *seeing the faith of them*—Luke included the faith of the man who was paralyzed. (He used *auton* (αυτων) and not *touton* (τουτων). *Touton* would have meant just the four on the roof.) Healing is primarily a faith proposition for the one seeking healing, not the one who is delivering it.

The better question is: Why don't those in the hospitals seek out the hand of the Lord like the woman with the issue of blood and blind Bartemaeus?

Question:

Weren't all of Jesus' healings instantaneous?

No. In one account, some people brought a blind man to him to heal (Jn 8:22-25). He spit on the man's eyes and laid his hands on him, then asked him what he saw. The man said, "I see men as trees, walking." The man, apparently, wasn't completely healed. Jesus laid his hands on the man again, and his sight was then fully restored.

Another time, ten lepers, standing off from the crowd because of their leprosy, called out to him for healing. He looked up and said, "Go, show yourselves to the priests." Luke wrote that they were healed as they withdrew. Their healing came about gradually.

In another instance, a nobleman sought healing for his son (Jn 4:49-53). Jesus told him, "Go your way, your son lives." When the nobleman made it home, he found that his son had been healed. The account indicates that his son began to amend, a gradual process, when Jesus first spoke to the man.

Question:

Can healings be lost?

Yes. Healing is a spiritual operation that is rooted in faith. If a man falls out of faith, he can lose it. Peter's walk on the water shows this. Jesus bid him to come and he got out of the boat and began walking on the water. While walking to Jesus, Peter saw the strong winds, got scared, and got out of faith. Jesus had to pull him up from sinking, asking him, "Why did you doubt?" Peter's doubt had stopped the flow of God's power.

After Jesus had healed the man at the pool of Bethesda, he ran into him in the temple and told him, "Don't sin lest a worse thing come on you." Though this man had been healed, Jesus told him that his last state could be worse than his first if he got out of faith and sinned against God.

Finally, James instructs believers to resist the devil so that he will flee (Jas 4:7). The implication is that if the believer doesn't stand in faith in the Word, the devil won't leave.

Question:

Are prayer requests for someone's healing scriptural?

The Word shows us different kinds of prayer for different kinds of requests, but it doesn't have anywhere in it the type of prayer requests for healing that we commonly see in churches today. That's because faith doesn't work by proxy.

Except for a few instances in the Gospels, the Word shows that people are expected to exercise faith for their own situations. In the few instances where someone was able to procure healing on behalf of someone else, the one requesting prayer or the laying on of hands had a special relationship with the sick one. Jairus asked for his little girl, the nobleman for his little boy. The centurion asked for his servant, over whom he exercised authority.

For the not-so-ordinary miracles under Paul's ministry (Acts 19:11), there's no record of anyone standing in proxy for anyone else. People, in fact, took aprons off of Paul and laid them on the sick. These situations were likely consistent with the roof-top account in Luke where the paralyzed one exercised his own faith to be healed.

A prayer request in line with scripture would ask that people pray that the sick believer's eyes be enlightened to know and understand all the blessings that God has already given us in Christ Jesus and the power toward us who believe (Eph 1:18-19). Healing has already been provided to us in Christ. But we must know and understand what riches we have in order to enjoy them.

Question:

What about lingering symptoms?

In a word, they're irrelevant. When God appeared to Abraham (Abram then) and preached that all nations would be blessed through him, Abraham knew that his body, being ninety-nine years old, was dead and that Sarah was barren. But he didn't look to those things. He looked only to the promise; he was fully persuaded that what God had declared him to be would come to pass.

After some relief, some shift their focus from he bore our sicknesses to their improved condition ("I'm much better now so I know that I'll recover.") and they sink like Peter did in the sea of Galilee. They replaced their reliance on the revealed truth to conditions in the natural. Abraham's faith was rewarded because he didn't take his eye off of God's promise. Even when God told him to sacrifice Isaac on an altar, Abraham still knew that all nations would be blessed through him because God had said it.

Question:

I'm still not too sure about Jesus bearing my sicknesses. Can I go ahead and pray for my healing anyway?

The fully persuaded believer is rewarded; the double-minded one is not. When God preached the Gospel to Abraham, Abraham could have kept his eyes on his flesh. He could have looked to his body, well past the age of producing a child, and Sarah's barren womb. If he had, the promise never would have been fulfilled. James wrote that if a man wavers on the viability of God's promises, that man shouldn't expect to receive anything from the Lord.

Peter's walking on the water also shows the hard truth of double-mindedness. One night the disciples had left Jesus to pray in the mountains while they sailed ahead to the other side of the sea. In the middle of their trip, a squall hit and they saw what they thought was a ghost about to pass them by. Jesus said, "It's me. Don't be afraid." Peter, seeing it was Jesus, said, "Lord, if it is you, bid me to come out on the water." Jesus said, "Come." Peter jumped over the ship's railing and began walking on the water to the Lord. Seeing the strong winds, he got scared and immediately began sinking.

"Save me!" Jesus caught him and, instead of congratulating him on his walk, rebuked him, "Puny faith! Why did you doubt?" (ἐδισταζω – doubleminded). He had taken his eyes off of the word and that shut off the power of God. Only those who walk in the same steps of Abraham get to receive the fulfillment of God's promises (Rom 4:12).

Scriptures

Old Testament

Genesis

2:7 – And the LORD God formed man of the dust of the ground, and breathed into his nostrils the breath of life; and man became a living soul.

2:25 – And they were both naked, the man and his wife, and were not ashamed.

3:7 – And the eyes of them both were opened, and they knew that they were naked; and they sewed fig leaves together, and made themselves aprons.

Exodus

7:15 – Get thee unto Pharaoh in the morning; lo, he goeth out unto the water; and thou shalt stand by the river's brink against he come; and the rod which was turned to a serpent shalt thou take in thine hand.

15:26 – And said, If thou wilt diligently hearken to the voice of the LORD thy God, and wilt do that which is right in his sight, and wilt give ear to his commandments, and keep all his statutes, I will put none of these diseases upon thee, which I have brought upon the Egyptians: for I am the LORD that healeth thee.

22:22 – Ye shall not afflict any widow, or fatherless child.

23:25 – And ye shall serve the LORD your God, and he shall bless thy bread, and thy water; and I will take sickness away from the midst of thee.

23:26 – There shall nothing cast their young, nor be barren, in thy land: the number of thy days I will fulfil.
40:13 – And thou shalt put upon Aaron the holy garments, and anoint him, and sanctify him; that he may minister unto me in the priest's office.
40:14 – And thou shalt bring his sons, and clothe them with coats:
40:15 – And thou shalt anoint them, as thou didst anoint their father, that they may minister unto me in the priest's office: for their anointing shall surely be an everlasting priesthood throughout their generations.

Leviticus

4:24 – And he shall lay his hand upon the head of the goat, and kill it in the place where they kill the burnt offering before the LORD: it is a sin offering.
14:1 – And the LORD spake unto Moses, saying,
14:2 – This shall be the law of the leper in the day of his cleansing: He shall be brought unto the priest:
14:3 – And the priest shall go forth out of the camp; and the priest shall look, and, behold, if the plague of leprosy be healed in the leper;
14:4 – Then shall the priest command to take for him that is to be cleansed two birds alive and clean, and cedar wood, and scarlet, and hyssop:
14:5 – And the priest shall command that one of the birds be killed in an earthen vessel over running water:
14:6 – As for the living bird, he shall take it, and the cedar wood, and the scarlet, and the hyssop, and shall

dip them and the living bird in the blood of the bird that was killed over the running water:

14:7 – And he shall sprinkle upon him that is to be cleansed from the leprosy seven times, and shall pronounce him clean, and shall let the living bird loose into the open field.

16:22 – And the goat shall bear upon him all their iniquities unto a land not inhabited: and he shall let go the goat in the wilderness.

Numbers

16:48 – And he stood between the dead and the living; and the plague was stayed.

Deuteronomy

7:15 – And the LORD will take away from thee all sickness, and will put none of the evil diseases of Egypt, which thou knowest, upon thee; but will lay them upon all them that hate thee.

25:4 – Thou shalt not muzzle the ox when he treadeth out the corn.

28:1 – And it shall come to pass, if thou shalt hearken diligently unto the voice of the LORD thy God, to observe and to do all his commandments which I command thee this day, that the LORD thy God will set thee on high above all nations of the earth:

28:2 – And all these blessings shall come on thee, and overtake thee, if thou shalt hearken unto the voice of the LORD thy God.

28:3 – Blessed shalt thou be in the city, and blessed shalt thou be in the field.

28:4 – Blessed shall be the fruit of thy body, and the fruit of thy ground, and the fruit of thy cattle, the increase of thy kine, and the flocks of thy sheep.

28:5 – Blessed shall be thy basket and thy store.

28:6 – Blessed shalt thou be when thou comest in, and blessed shalt thou be when thou goest out.

28:7 – The LORD shall cause thine enemies that rise up against thee to be smitten before thy face: they shall come out against thee one way, and flee before thee seven ways.

28:8 – The LORD shall command the blessing upon thee in thy storehouses, and in all that thou settest thine hand unto; and he shall bless thee in the land which the LORD thy God giveth thee.

28:9 – The LORD shall establish thee an holy people unto himself, as he hath sworn unto thee, if thou shalt keep the commandments of the LORD thy God, and walk in his ways.

28:10 – And all people of the earth shall see that thou art called by the name of the LORD; and they shall be afraid of thee.

28:11 – And the LORD shall make thee plenteous in goods, in the fruit of thy body, and in the fruit of thy cattle, and in the fruit of thy ground, in the land which the LORD sware unto thy fathers to give thee.

28:12 – The LORD shall open unto thee his good treasure, the heaven to give the rain unto thy land in his season, and to bless all the work of thine hand: and thou shalt lend unto many nations, and thou shalt not borrow.

28:13 – And the LORD shall make thee the head, and not the tail; and thou shalt be above only, and thou shalt not be beneath; if that thou hearken unto the commandments of the LORD thy God, which I command thee this day, to observe and to do them:

28:14 – And thou shalt not go aside from any of the words which I command thee this day, to the right hand, or to the left, to go after other gods to serve them.

28:15 – But it shall come to pass, if thou wilt not hearken unto the voice of the LORD thy God, to observe to do all his commandments and his statutes which I command thee this day; that all these curses shall come upon thee, and overtake thee:

28:21 – The LORD shall make the pestilence cleave unto thee, until he have consumed thee from off the land, whither thou goest to possess it.

28:22 – The LORD shall smite thee with a consumption, and with a fever, and with an inflammation, and with an extreme burning, and with the sword, and with blasting, and with mildew; and they shall pursue thee until thou perish.

28:27 – The LORD will smite thee with the botch of Egypt, and with the hemorrhoids, and with the scab, and with the itch, whereof thou canst not be healed.

28:28 – The LORD shall smite thee with madness, and blindness, and astonishment of heart:

28:59 – Then the LORD will make thy plagues wonderful, and the plagues of thy seed, even great plagues, and of long continuance, and sore sicknesses, and of long continuance.

28:61 – Also every sickness, and every plague, which is not written in the book of this law, them will the LORD bring upon thee, until thou be destroyed.

1 Kings

8:11 – So that the priests could not stand to minister because of the cloud: for the glory of the LORD had filled the house of the LORD.
17:17 – And it came to pass after these things, that the son of the woman, the mistress of the house, fell sick; and his sickness was so sore, that there was no breath left in him.
17:18 – And she said unto Elijah, What have I to do with thee, O thou man of God? art thou come unto me to call my sin to remembrance, and to slay my son?
17:19 – And he said unto her, Give me thy son. And he took him out of her bosom, and carried him up into a loft, where he abode, and laid him upon his own bed.
17:20 – And he cried unto the Lord, and said, O Lord my God, hast thou also brought evil upon the widow with whom I sojourn, by slaying her son?
17:21 – And he stretched himself upon the child three times, and cried unto the Lord, and said, O Lord my God, I pray thee, let this child's soul come into him again.
17:22 – And the LORD heard the voice of Elijah; and the soul of the child came into him again, and he revived.

17:23 – And Elijah took the child, and brought him down out of the chamber into the house, and delivered him unto his mother: and Elijah said, See, thy son liveth.

17:24 – And the woman said to Elijah, Now by this I know that thou art a man of God, and that the word of the Lord in thy mouth is truth.

2 Kings

1:2 – And Ahaziah fell down through a lattice in his upper chamber that was in Samaria, and was sick: and he sent messengers, and said unto them, Go, enquire of Baalzebub the god of Ekron whether I shall recover of this disease.

5:3 –And she said unto her mistress, Would God my lord were with the prophet that is in Samaria! for he would recover him of his leprosy.

5:10 – And Elisha sent a messenger unto him, saying, Go and wash in Jordan seven times, and thy flesh shall come again to thee, and thou shalt be clean.

5:14 – Then went he down, and dipped himself seven times in Jordan, according to the saying of the man of God: and his flesh came again like unto the flesh of a little child, and he was clean.

8:8 – And the king said unto Hazael, Take a present in thine hand, and go, meet the man of God, and enquire of the LORD by him, saying, Shall I recover of this disease?

13:20 – And Elisha died, and they buried him. And the bands of the Moabites invaded the land at the coming in of the year.

13:21 – And it came to pass, as they were burying a man, that, behold, they spied a band of men; and they cast the man into the sepulchre of Elisha: and when the man was let down, and touched the bones of Elisha, he revived, and stood up on his feet.

2 Chronicles

5:14 – So that the priests could not stand to minister by reason of the cloud: for the glory of the LORD had filled the house of God.

16:12 – And Asa in the thirty and ninth year of his reign was diseased in his feet, until his disease was exceeding great: yet in his disease he sought not to the LORD, but to the physicians.

21:15 – And thou shalt have great sickness by disease of thy bowels, until thy bowels fall out by reason of the sickness day by day.

Job

33:19 – He is chastened also with pain upon his bed, and the multitude of his bones with strong pain:

Psalms

22:1 – My God, my God, why hast thou forsaken me? why art thou so far from helping me, and from the words of my roaring?

22:2 – O my God, I cry in the daytime, but thou hearest me not; and in the night season, and am not silent.

22:6 – But I am a worm, and no man; a reproach of men, and despised of the people.

22:14 – I am poured out like water, and all my bones are out of joint: my heart is like wax; it is melted in the midst of my bowels.

22:15 –My strength is dried up like a potsherd; and my tongue cleaveth to my jaws; and thou has brought me into the dust of death.

105:37 – He brought them forth also with silver and gold: and there was not one feeble person among their tribes.

Ecclesiastes

12:12 – And further, by these, my son, be admonished: of making many books there is no end; and much study is a weariness of the flesh.

Isaiah

38:21 – For Isaiah had said, Let them take a lump of figs, and lay it for a plaster upon the boil, and he shall recover.

46:4 – And even to your old age I am he; and even to hoar hairs will I carry you: I have made, and I will bear; even I will carry, and will deliver you.

46:7 – They bear him upon the shoulder, they carry him, and set him in his place, and he standeth; from his place shall he not remove: yea, one shall cry unto him, yet can he not answer, nor save him out of his trouble.

52:14 – As many were astonied at thee; his visage was so marred more than any man, and his form more than the sons of men:

53:3 – He is despised and rejected of men; a man of sorrows, and acquainted with grief: and we hid as it were our faces from him; he was despised, and we esteemed him not.

53:4 – Surely he hath borne our griefs, and carried our sorrows: yet we did esteem him stricken, smitten of God, and afflicted.

53:5 – But he was wounded for our transgressions, he was bruised for our iniquities: the chastisement of our peace was upon him; and with his stripes we are healed.

53:12 – Therefore will I divide him a portion with the great, and he shall divide the spoil with the strong; because he hath poured out his soul unto death: and he was numbered with the transgressors; and he bare the sin of many, and made intercession for the transgressors.

Hosea

5:13 – When Ephraim saw his sickness, and Judah saw his wound, then went Ephraim to the Assyrian, and sent to king Jareb: yet could he not heal you, nor cure you of your wound.

Zechariah

3:1 – And he shewed me Joshua the high priest standing before the angel of the LORD, and Satan standing at his right hand to resist him.

New Testament

Matthew

3:16 – And Jesus, when he was baptized, went up straightway out of the water: and, lo, the heavens were opened unto him, and he saw the Spirit of God descending like a dove, and lighting upon him:

4:24 – And his fame went throughout all Syria: and they brought unto him all sick people that were taken with divers diseases and torments, and those which were possessed with devils, and those which were lunatick, and those that had the palsy; and he healed them.

8:5 – And when Jesus was entered into Capernaum, there came unto him a centurion, beseeching him,

8:6 – And saying, Lord, my servant lieth at home sick of the palsy, grievously tormented.

8:7 – And Jesus saith unto him, I will come and heal him.

8:8 – The centurion answered and said, Lord, I am not worthy that thou shouldest come under my roof: but speak the word only, and my servant shall be healed.

8:9 – For I am a man under authority, having soldiers under me: and I say to this man, Go, and he goeth; and to another, Come, and he cometh; and to my servant, Do this, and he doeth it.

8:10 – When Jesus heard it, he marvelled, and said to them that followed, Verily I say unto you, I have not found so great faith, no, not in Israel.

8:11 – And I say unto you, That many shall come from the east and west, and shall sit down with Abraham, and Isaac, and Jacob, in the kingdom of heaven.

8:12 – But the children of the kingdom shall be cast out into outer darkness: there shall be weeping and gnashing of teeth.

8:13 – And Jesus said unto the centurion, Go thy way; and as thou hast believed, so be it done unto thee. And his servant was healed in the selfsame hour.

8:16 – When the even was come, they brought unto him many that were possessed with devils: and he cast out the spirits with his word, and healed all that were sick:

8:17 – That it might be fulfilled which was spoken by Esaias the prophet, saying, Himself took our infirmities, and bare our sicknesses.

9:35 – And Jesus went about all the cities and villages, teaching in their synagogues, and preaching the gospel of the kingdom, and healing every sickness and every disease among the people.

10:5 – These twelve Jesus sent forth, and commanded them, saying, Go not into the way of the Gentiles, and into any city of the Samaritans enter ye not:

10:6 – But go rather to the lost sheep of the house of Israel.

10:7 – And as ye go, preach, saying, The kingdom of heaven is at hand.

10:8 – Heal the sick, cleanse the lepers, raise the dead, cast out devils: freely ye have received, freely give.

12:9 – And when he was departed thence, he went into their synagogue:

12:10 – And, behold, there was a man which had his hand withered. And they asked him, saying, Is it lawful to heal on the sabbath days? that they might accuse him.

12:11 – And he said unto them, What man shall there be among you, that shall have one sheep, and if it fall into a pit on the sabbath day, will he not lay hold on it, and lift it out?

12:12 – How much then is a man better than a sheep? Wherefore it is lawful to do well on the sabbath days.

12:13 – Then saith he to the man, Stretch forth thine hand. And he stretched it forth; and it was restored whole, like as the other.

12:14 – Then the Pharisees went out, and held a council against him, how they might destroy him.

12:15 – But when Jesus knew it, he withdrew himself from thence: and great multitudes followed him, and he healed them all;

12:16 – And charged them that they should not make him known:

12:17 – That it might be fulfilled which was spoken by Esaias the prophet, saying,

12:18 – Behold my servant, whom I have chosen; my beloved, in whom my soul is well pleased: I will put my spirit upon him, and he shall shew judgment to the Gentiles.

12:22 - Then was brought unto him one possessed with a devil, blind, and dumb: and he healed him, insomuch that the blind and dumb both spake and saw.

12:40 – For as Jonas was three days and three nights in the whale's belly; so shall the Son of man be three days and three nights in the heart of the earth.

13:15 – For this people's heart is waxed gross, and their ears are dull of hearing, and their eyes they have closed; lest at any time they should see with their eyes, and hear with their ears, and should understand with their heart, and should be converted, and I should heal them.

14:34 – And when they were gone over, they came into the land of Gennesaret.

14:35 – And when the men of that place had knowledge of him, they sent out into all that country round about, and brought unto him all that were diseased;

14:36 – And besought him that they might only touch the hem of his garment: and as many as touched were made perfectly whole.

15:24 – But he answered and said, I am not sent but unto the lost sheep of the house of Israel.

15:28 – Then Jesus answered and said unto her, O woman, great is thy faith: be it unto thee even as thou wilt. And her daughter was made whole from that very hour.

21:16 – And said unto him, Hearest thou what these say? And Jesus saith unto them, Yea; have ye never read, Out of the mouth of babes and sucklings thou hast perfected praise?

21:42 – Jesus saith unto them, Did ye never read in the scriptures, The stone which the builders rejected, the same is become the head of the corner: this is the Lord's doing, and it is marvellous in our eyes?

24:1 – And Jesus went out, and departed from the temple: and his disciples came to him for to shew him the buildings of the temple.

27:43 – He trusted in God; let him deliver him now, if he will have him: for he said, I am the Son of God.

28.18 – And Jesus came and spake unto them, saying, All power is given unto me in heaven and in earth.

Mark

1:34 – And he healed many that were sick of divers diseases, and cast out many devils; and suffered not the devils to speak, because they knew him.

2:1 – And again he entered into Capernaum after some days; and it was noised that he was in the house.

2:2 – And straightway many were gathered together, insomuch that there was no room to receive them, no, not so much as about the door: and he preached the word unto them.

3:11 – And unclean spirits, when they saw him, fell down before him, and cried, saying, Thou art the Son of God.

3:12 – And he straitly charged them that they should not make him known.

3:14 – And he ordained twelve, that they should be with him, and that he might send them forth to preach,

5:1 – And they came over unto the other side of the sea, into the country of the Gadarenes.

5:2 – And when he was come out of the ship, immediately there met him out of the tombs a man with an unclean spirit,

5:3 – Who had his dwelling among the tombs; and no man could bind him, no, not with chains:

5:4 – Because that he had been often bound with fetters and chains, and the chains had been plucked asunder by him, and the fetters broken in pieces: neither could any man tame him.

5:5 – And always, night and day, he was in the mountains, and in the tombs, crying, and cutting himself with stones.

5:6 – But when he saw Jesus afar off, he ran and worshipped him,

5:7 – And cried with a loud voice, and said, What have I to do with thee, Jesus, thou Son of the most high God? I adjure thee by God, that thou torment me not.

5:8 – For he said unto him, Come out of the man, thou unclean spirit.

5:9 – And he asked him, What is thy name? And he answered, saying, My name is Legion: for we are many.

5:10 – And he besought him much that he would not send them away out of the country.

5:11 – Now there was there nigh unto the mountains a great herd of swine feeding.

5:12 – And all the devils besought him, saying, Send us into the swine, that we may enter into them.

5:13 – And forthwith Jesus gave them leave. And the unclean spirits went out, and entered into the swine: and the herd ran violently down a steep place into the sea, (they were about two thousand;) and were choked in the sea.

5:14 – And they that fed the swine fled, and told it in the city, and in the country. And they went out to see what it was that was done.

5:15 – And they come to Jesus, and see him that was possessed with the devil, and had the legion, sitting, and clothed, and in his right mind: and they were afraid.

5:16 – And they that saw it told them how it befell to him that was possessed with the devil, and also concerning the swine.

5:17 – And they began to pray him to depart out of their coasts.

5:22 – And, behold, there cometh one of the rulers of the synagogue, Jairus by name; and when he saw him, he fell at his feet,

5:23 – And besought him greatly, saying, My little daughter lieth at the point of death: I pray thee, come and lay thy hands on her, that she may be healed; and she shall live.

5:24 – And Jesus went with him; and much people followed him, and thronged him.

5:25 – And a certain woman, which had an issue of blood twelve years,

5:26 – And had suffered many things of many physicians, and had spent all that she had, and was nothing bettered, but rather grew worse,

5:27 – When she had heard of Jesus, came in the press behind, and touched his garment.

5:28 – For she said, If I may touch but his clothes, I shall be whole.

5:29 – And straightway the fountain of her blood was dried up; and she felt in her body that she was healed of that plague.

5:30 – And Jesus, immediately knowing in himself that virtue had gone out of him, turned him about in the press, and said, Who touched my clothes?

6:56 – And whithersoever he entered, into villages, or cities, or country, they laid the sick in the streets, and besought him that they might touch if it were but the border of his garment: and as many as touched him were made whole.

6:4 – But Jesus said unto them, A prophet is not without honour, but in his own country, and among his own kin, and in his own house.

And he could there do no mighty work, save that he laid his hands upon a few sick folk, and healed them.

8:22 – And he cometh to Bethsaida; and they bring a blind man unto him, and besought him to touch him.

8:23 – And he took the blind man by the hand, and led him out of the town; and when he had spit on his eyes, and put his hands upon him, he asked him if he saw ought.

8:24 – And he looked up, and said, I see men as trees, walking.

8:25 – After that he put his hands again upon his eyes, and made him look up: and he was restored, and saw every man clearly.

9:14 – And when he came to his disciples, he saw a great multitude about them, and the scribes questioning with them.

9:15 – And straightway all the people, when they beheld him, were greatly amazed, and running to him saluted him.

9:16 – And he asked the scribes, What question ye with them?

9:17 – And one of the multitude answered and said, Master, I have brought unto thee my son, which hath a dumb spirit;

9:18 – And wheresoever he taketh him, he teareth him: and he foameth, and gnasheth with his teeth, and pineth away: and I spake to thy disciples that they should cast him out; and they could not.

9:19 – He answereth him, and saith, O faithless generation, how long shall I be with you? how long shall I suffer you? bring him unto me.

9:20 – And they brought him unto him: and when he saw him, straightway the spirit tare him; and he fell on the ground, and wallowed foaming.

9:21 – And he asked his father, How long is it ago since this came unto him? And he said, Of a child.

9:22 – And ofttimes it hath cast him into the fire, and into the waters, to destroy him: but if thou canst do any thing, have compassion on us, and help us.

9:23 – Jesus said unto him, If thou canst believe, all things are possible to him that believeth.

9:24 – And straightway the father of the child cried out, and said with tears, Lord, I believe; help thou mine unbelief.

9:25 – When Jesus saw that the people came running together, he rebuked the foul spirit, saying unto him,

Thou dumb and deaf spirit, I charge thee, come out of him, and enter no more into him.

9:26 – And the spirit cried, and rent him sore, and came out of him: and he was as one dead; insomuch that many said, He is dead.

9:27 – But Jesus took him by the hand, and lifted him up; and he arose.

11:11 – And Jesus entered into Jerusalem, and into the temple: and when he had looked round about upon all things, and now the eventide was come, he went out unto Bethany with the twelve.

11:24 – Therefore I say unto you, What things soever ye desire, when ye pray, believe that ye receive them, and ye shall have them.

16:18 – They shall take up serpents; and if they drink any deadly thing, it shall not hurt them; they shall lay hands on the sick, and they shall recover.

16:20 – And they went forth, and preached every where, the Lord working with them, and confirming the word with signs following. Amen.

Luke

1:3 – It seemed good to me also, having had perfect understanding of all things from the very first, to write unto thee in order, most excellent Theophilus,

4:18 – The Spirit of the Lord is upon me, because he hath anointed me to preach the gospel to the poor; he hath sent me to heal the brokenhearted, to preach deliverance to the captives, and recovering of sight to the blind, to set at liberty them that are bruised,

4:19 – To preach the acceptable year of the Lord.

4:25 – But I tell you of a truth, many widows were in Israel in the days of Elias, when the heaven was shut up three years and six months, when great famine was throughout all the land;

4:26 – But unto none of them was Elias sent, save unto Sarepta, a city of Sidon, unto a woman that was a widow.

4:30 – But he passing through the midst of them went his way,

4:31 – And came down to Capernaum, a city of Galilee, and taught them on the sabbath days.

4:32 – And they were astonished at his doctrine: for his word was with power.

4:33 – And in the synagogue there was a man, which had a spirit of an unclean devil, and cried out with a loud voice,

4:34 – Saying, Let us alone; what have we to do with thee, thou Jesus of Nazareth? art thou come to destroy us? I know thee who thou art; the Holy One of God.

4:35 – And Jesus rebuked him, saying, Hold thy peace, and come out of him. And when the devil had thrown him in the midst, he came out of him, and hurt him not.

4:38 – And he arose out of the synagogue, and entered into Simon's house. And Simon's wife's mother was taken with a great fever; and they besought him for her.

4:39 – And he stood over her, and rebuked the fever; and it left her: and immediately she arose and ministered unto them.

4:40 – Now when the sun was setting, all they that had any sick with divers diseases brought them unto him;

and he laid his hands on every one of them, and healed them.

4:41 – And devils also came out of many, crying out, and saying, Thou art Christ the Son of God. And he rebuking them suffered them not to speak: for they knew that he was Christ.

5:15 But so much the more went there a fame abroad of him: and great multitudes came together to hear, and to be healed by him of their infirmities.

5:17 – And it came to pass on a certain day, as he was teaching, that there were Pharisees and doctors of the law sitting by, which were come out of every town of Galilee, and Judaea, and Jerusalem: and the power of the Lord was present to heal them.

6:17 – And he came down with them, and stood in the plain, and the company of his disciples, and a great multitude of people out of all Judaea and Jerusalem, and from the sea coast of Tyre and Sidon, which came to hear him, and to be healed of their diseases;

6:18 – And they that were vexed with unclean spirits: and they were healed.

6:19 – And the whole multitude sought to touch him: for there went virtue out of him, and healed them all.

7:7 – Wherefore neither thought I myself worthy to come unto thee: but say in a word, and my servant shall be healed.

7:46 – My head with oil thou didst not anoint: but this woman hath anointed my feet with ointment.

8:2 – And certain women, which had been healed of evil spirits and infirmities, Mary called Magdalene, out of whom went seven devils,

8:26 – And they arrived at the country of the Gadarenes, which is over against Galilee.

8:27 – And when he went forth to land, there met him out of the city a certain man, which had devils long time, and ware no clothes, neither abode in any house, but in the tombs.

8:28 – When he saw Jesus, he cried out, and fell down before him, and with a loud voice said, What have I to do with thee, Jesus, thou Son of God most high? I beseech thee, torment me not.

8:47 – And when the woman saw that she was not hid, she came trembling, and falling down before him, she declared unto him before all the people for what cause she had touched him, and how she was healed immediately.

9:1 – Then he called his twelve disciples together, and gave them power and authority over all devils, and to cure diseases.

9:2 – And he sent them to preach the kingdom of God, and to heal the sick.

9:42 – And as he was yet a coming, the devil threw him down, and tare him. And Jesus rebuked the unclean spirit, and healed the child, and delivered him again to his father.

9:46 – Then there arose a reasoning among them, which of them should be greatest.

10:1 – After these things the Lord appointed other seventy also, and sent them two and two before his face into every city and place, whither he himself would come.

13:11 – And, behold, there was a woman which had a spirit of infirmity eighteen years, and was bowed together, and could in no wise lift up herself.

13:12 – And when Jesus saw her, he called her to him, and said unto her, Woman, thou art loosed from thine infirmity.

13:13 – And he laid his hands on her: and immediately she was made straight, and glorified God.

13:14 – And the ruler of the synagogue answered with indignation, because that Jesus had healed on the sabbath day, and said unto the people, There are six days in which men ought to work: in them therefore come and be healed, and not on the sabbath day.

13:15 – The Lord then answered him, and said, Thou hypocrite, doth not each one of you on the sabbath loose his ox or his ass from the stall, and lead him away to watering?

13:16 – And ought not this woman, being a daughter of Abraham, whom Satan hath bound, lo, these eighteen years, be loosed from this bond on the sabbath day?

14:4 – And they held their peace. And he took him, and healed him, and let him go;

17:14 – And when he saw them, he said unto them, Go shew yourselves unto the priests. And it came to pass, that, as they went, they were cleansed.

17:15 – And one of them, when he saw that he was healed, turned back, and with a loud voice glorified God,

22:51 – And Jesus answered and said, Suffer ye thus far. And he touched his ear, and healed him.

22:44 – And being in an agony he prayed more earnestly: and his sweat was as it were great drops of blood falling down to the ground.

24:49 – And, behold, I send the promise of my Father upon you: but tarry ye in the city of Jerusalem, until ye be endued with power from on high.

John

1:8 – He was not that Light, but was sent to bear witness of that Light.

1:33 – And I knew him not: but he that sent me to baptize with water, the same said unto me, Upon whom thou shalt see the Spirit descending, and remaining on him, the same is he which baptizeth with the Holy Ghost.

2:11 – This beginning of miracles did Jesus in Cana of Galilee, and manifested forth his glory; and his disciples believed on him.

3:34 – For he whom God hath sent speaketh the words of God: for God giveth not the Spirit by measure unto him.

4:46 – So Jesus came again into Cana of Galilee, where he made the water wine. And there was a certain nobleman, whose son was sick at Capernaum.

4:47 – When he heard that Jesus was come out of Judaea into Galilee, he went unto him, and besought him that he would come down, and heal his son: for he was at the point of death.

4:48 – Then said Jesus unto him, Except ye see signs and wonders, ye will not believe.

4:49 – The nobleman saith unto him, Sir, come down ere my child die.

4:50 – Jesus saith unto him, Go thy way; thy son liveth. And the man believed the word that Jesus had spoken unto him, and he went his way.

4:51 – And as he was now going down, his servants met him, and told him, saying, Thy son liveth.

4:52 – Then enquired he of them the hour when he began to amend. And they said unto him, Yesterday at the seventh hour the fever left him.

4:53 – So the father knew that it was at the same hour, in the which Jesus said unto him, Thy son liveth: and himself believed, and his whole house.

5:1 – After this there was a feast of the Jews; and Jesus went up to Jerusalem.

5:2 – Now there is at Jerusalem by the sheep market a pool, which is called in the Hebrew tongue Bethesda, having five porches.

5:3 – In these lay a great multitude of impotent folk, of blind, halt, withered, waiting for the moving of the water.

5:4 – For an angel went down at a certain season into the pool, and troubled the water: whosoever then first after the troubling of the water stepped in was made whole of whatsoever disease he had.

5:5 – And a certain man was there, which had an infirmity thirty and eight years.

5:6 – When Jesus saw him lie, and knew that he had been now a long time in that case, he saith unto him, Wilt thou be made whole?

5:7 – The impotent man answered him, Sir, I have no man, when the water is troubled, to put me into the pool: but while I am coming, another steppeth down before me.

5:8 – Jesus saith unto him, Rise, take up thy bed, and walk.

5:9 – And immediately the man was made whole, and took up his bed, and walked: and on the same day was the sabbath.

5:13 – And he that was healed wist not who it was: for Jesus had conveyed himself away, a multitude being in that place.

5:14 – Afterward Jesus findeth him in the temple, and said unto him, Behold, thou art made whole: sin no more, lest a worse thing come unto thee.

5:16 – And therefore did the Jews persecute Jesus, and sought to slay him, because he had done these things on the sabbath day.

5:17 – But Jesus answered them, My Father worketh hitherto, and I work.

5:18 – Therefore the Jews sought the more to kill him, because he not only had broken the sabbath, but said also that God was his Father, making himself equal with God.

5:19 – Then answered Jesus and said unto them, Verily, verily, I say unto you, The Son can do nothing of himself, but what he seeth the Father do: for what things soever he doeth, these also doeth the Son likewise.

6:34 – Then said they unto him, Lord, evermore give us this bread.

7:14 – Now about the midst of the feast Jesus went up into the temple, and taught.

8:12 – Then spake Jesus again unto them, saying, I am the light of the world: he that followeth me shall not walk in darkness, but shall have the light of life.

8:34 – Jesus answered them, Verily, verily, I say unto you, Whosoever committeth sin is the servant of sin.

8:36 – If the Son therefore shall make you free, ye shall be free indeed.

9:1 – And as Jesus passed by, he saw a man which was blind from his birth.

9:2 – And his disciples asked him, saying, Master, who did sin, this man, or his parents, that he was born blind?

9:3 – Jesus answered, Neither hath this man sinned, nor his parents: but that the works of God should be made manifest in him.

9:4 – I must work the works of him that sent me, while it is day: the night cometh, when no man can work.

9:5 – As long as I am in the world, I am the light of the world.

9:6 – When he had thus spoken, he spat on the ground, and made clay of the spittle, and he anointed the eyes of the blind man with the clay,

9:7 – And said unto him, Go, wash in the pool of Siloam, (which is by interpretation, Sent.) He went his way therefore, and washed, and came seeing.

10:23 – And Jesus walked in the temple in Solomon's porch.

11:1 – Now a certain man was sick, named Lazarus, of Bethany, the town of Mary and her sister Martha.

11:2 – (It was that Mary which anointed the Lord with ointment, and wiped his feet with her hair, whose brother Lazarus was sick.)

11:3 – Therefore his sisters sent unto him, saying, Lord, behold, he whom thou lovest is sick.

11:4 – When Jesus heard that, he said, This sickness is not unto death, but for the glory of God, that the Son of God might be glorified thereby.

11:5 – Now Jesus loved Martha, and her sister, and Lazarus.

11:6 – When he had heard therefore that he was sick, he abode two days still in the same place where he was.

11:7 – Then after that saith he to his disciples, Let us go into Judaea again.

11:8 – His disciples say unto him, Master, the Jews of late sought to stone thee; and goest thou thither again?

11:9 – Jesus answered, Are there not twelve hours in the day? If any man walk in the day, he stumbleth not, because he seeth the light of this world.

11:10 – But if a man walk in the night, he stumbleth, because there is no light in him.

11:11 – These things said he: and after that he saith unto them, Our friend Lazarus sleepeth; but I go, that I may awake him out of sleep.

11:12 – Then said his disciples, Lord, if he sleep, he shall do well.

11:13 – Howbeit Jesus spake of his death: but they thought that he had spoken of taking of rest in sleep.

11:14 – Then said Jesus unto them plainly, Lazarus is dead.

11:15 – And I am glad for your sakes that I was not there, to the intent ye may believe; nevertheless let us go unto him.

11:16 – Then said Thomas, which is called Didymus, unto his fellow disciples, Let us also go, that we may die with him.

11:17 – Then when Jesus came, he found that he had lain in the grave four days already.

11:18 – Now Bethany was nigh unto Jerusalem, about fifteen furlongs off:

11:19 – And many of the Jews came to Martha and Mary, to comfort them concerning their brother.

11:20 – Then Martha, as soon as she heard that Jesus was coming, went and met him: but Mary sat still in the house.

11:21 – Then said Martha unto Jesus, Lord, if thou hadst been here, my brother had not died.

11:22 – But I know, that even now, whatsoever thou wilt ask of God, God will give it thee.

11:23 – Jesus saith unto her, Thy brother shall rise again.

11:24 – Martha saith unto him, I know that he shall rise again in the resurrection at the last day.

11:25 – Jesus said unto her, I am the resurrection, and the life: he that believeth in me, though he were dead, yet shall he live:

11:26 – And whosoever liveth and believeth in me shall never die. Believest thou this?

11:27 – She saith unto him, Yea, Lord: I believe that thou art the Christ, the Son of God, which should come into the world.

11:28 – And when she had so said, she went her way, and called Mary her sister secretly, saying, The Master is come, and calleth for thee.

11:29 – As soon as she heard that, she arose quickly, and came unto him.

11:30 – Now Jesus was not yet come into the town, but was in that place where Martha met him.

11:31 – The Jews then which were with her in the house, and comforted her, when they saw Mary, that she rose up hastily and went out, followed her, saying, She goeth unto the grave to weep there.

11:32 – Then when Mary was come where Jesus was, and saw him, she fell down at his feet, saying unto him, Lord, if thou hadst been here, my brother had not died.

11:33 – When Jesus therefore saw her weeping, and the Jews also weeping which came with her, he groaned in the spirit, and was troubled,

11:34 – And said, Where have ye laid him? They said unto him, Lord, come and see.

11:35 – Jesus wept.

11:36 – Then said the Jews, Behold how he loved him!

11:37 – And some of them said, Could not this man, which opened the eyes of the blind, have caused that even this man should not have died?

11:38 – Jesus therefore again groaning in himself cometh to the grave. It was a cave, and a stone lay upon it.

11:39 – Jesus said, Take ye away the stone. Martha, the sister of him that was dead, saith unto him, Lord, by this time he stinketh: for he hath been dead four days.

11:40 – Jesus saith unto her, Said I not unto thee, that, if thou wouldest believe, thou shouldest see the glory of God?

11:41 – Then they took away the stone from the place where the dead was laid. And Jesus lifted up his eyes, and said, Father, I thank thee that thou hast heard me.

11:42 – And I knew that thou hearest me always: but because of the people which stand by I said it, that they may believe that thou hast sent me.

11:43 – And when he thus had spoken, he cried with a loud voice, Lazarus, come forth.

11:44 – And he that was dead came forth, bound hand and foot with graveclothes: and his face was bound about with a napkin. Jesus saith unto them, Loose him, and let him go.

12:40 – He hath blinded their eyes, and hardened their heart; that they should not see with their eyes, nor understand with their heart, and be converted, and I should heal them.

13:31 – Therefore, when he was gone out, Jesus said, Now is the Son of man glorified, and God is glorified in him.

13:35 – By this shall all men know that ye are my disciples, if ye have love one to another.

13:36 – Simon Peter said unto him, Lord, whither goest thou? Jesus answered him, Whither I go, thou canst not follow me now; but thou shalt follow me afterwards.

14:31 – But that the world may know that I love the Father; and as the Father gave me commandment, even so I do. Arise, let us go hence.

16:2 – They shall put you out of the synagogues: yea, the time cometh, that whosoever killeth you will think that he doeth God service.

18:6 – As soon then as he had said unto them, I am he, they went backward, and fell to the ground.

20:22 – And when he had said this, he breathed on them, and saith unto them, Receive ye the Holy Ghost:

Acts

2:1 – And when the day of Pentecost was fully come, they were all with one accord in one place.

2:4 – And they were all filled with the Holy Ghost, and began to speak with other tongues, as the Spirit gave them utterance.

2:24 – Whom God hath raised up, having loosed the pains of death: because it was not possible that he should be holden of it.

3:1 – Now Peter and John went up together into the temple at the hour of prayer, being the ninth hour.

3:2 – And a certain man lame from his mother's womb was carried, whom they laid daily at the gate of the temple which is called Beautiful, to ask alms of them that entered into the temple;

3:3 – Who seeing Peter and John about to go into the temple asked an alms.

3:4 – And Peter, fastening his eyes upon him with John, said, Look on us.

3:5 – And he gave heed unto them, expecting to receive something of them.

3:6 – Then Peter said, Silver and gold have I none; but such as I have give I thee: In the name of Jesus Christ of Nazareth rise up and walk.

3:7 – And he took him by the right hand, and lifted him up: and immediately his feet and ankle bones received strength.

3:8 – And he leaping up stood, and walked, and entered with them into the temple, walking, and leaping, and praising God.

3:11 – And as the lame man which was healed held Peter and John, all the people ran together unto them in the porch that is called Solomon's, greatly wondering.

3:15 – And killed the Prince of life, whom God hath raised from the dead; whereof we are witnesses.

4:1 – And as they spake unto the people, the priests, and the captain of the temple, and the Sadducees, came upon them,

4:2 – Being grieved that they taught the people, and preached through Jesus the resurrection from the dead.

4:3 – And they laid hands on them, and put them in hold unto the next day: for it was now eventide.

4:4 – Howbeit many of them which heard the word believed; and the number of the men was about five thousand.

4:16 – Saying, What shall we do to these men? for that indeed a notable miracle hath been done by them is manifest to all them that dwell in Jerusalem; and we cannot deny it.

4:17 – But that it spread no further among the people, let us straitly threaten them, that they speak henceforth to no man in this name.

4:18 – And they called them, and commanded them not to speak at all nor teach in the name of Jesus.

4:22 – For the man was above forty years old, on whom this miracle of healing was shewed.

4:30 – By stretching forth thine hand to heal; and that signs and wonders may be done by the name of thy holy child Jesus.

5:15 – Insomuch that they brought forth the sick into the streets, and laid them on beds and couches, that at the least the shadow of Peter passing by might overshadow some of them.

5:16 – There came also a multitude out of the cities round about unto Jerusalem, bringing sick folks, and them which were vexed with unclean spirits: and they were healed every one.

5:41 – And they departed from the presence of the council, rejoicing that they were counted worthy to suffer shame for his name.

8:26 – And the angel of the Lord spake unto Philip, saying, Arise, and go toward the south unto the way that goeth down from Jerusalem unto Gaza, which is desert.

8:27 – And he arose and went: and, behold, a man of Ethiopia, an eunuch of great authority under Candace queen of the Ethiopians, who had the charge of all her treasure, and had come to Jerusalem for to worship,

8:28 – Was returning, and sitting in his chariot read Esaias the prophet.

8:29 – Then the Spirit said unto Philip, Go near, and join thyself to this chariot.

8:30 – And Philip ran thither to him, and heard him read the prophet Esaias, and said, Understandest thou what thou readest?

8:31 – And he said, How can I, except some man should guide me? And he desired Philip that he would come up and sit with him.

8:32 – The place of the scripture which he read was this, He was led as a sheep to the slaughter; and like a lamb dumb before his shearer, so opened he not his mouth:

8:33 – In his humiliation his judgment was taken away: and who shall declare his generation? for his life is taken from the earth.

8:34 – And the eunuch answered Philip, and said, I pray thee, of whom speaketh the prophet this? of himself, or of some other man?

8:35 – Then Philip opened his mouth, and began at the same scripture, and preached unto him Jesus.

9:34 – And Peter said unto him, Aeneas, Jesus Christ maketh thee whole: arise, and make thy bed. And he arose immediately.

10:38 – How God anointed Jesus of Nazareth with the Holy Ghost and with power: who went about doing good, and healing all that were oppressed of the devil; for God was with him.

13:1 – Now there were in the church that was at Antioch certain prophets and teachers; as Barnabas, and Simeon that was called Niger, and Lucius of Cyrene, and Manaen, which had been brought up with Herod the tetrarch, and Saul.

14:8 – And there sat a certain man at Lystra, impotent in his feet, being a cripple from his mother's womb, who never had walked:

14:9 – The same heard Paul speak: who steadfastly beholding him, and perceiving that he had faith to be healed,

14:10 – Said with a loud voice, Stand upright on thy feet. And he leaped and walked.

18:3 – And because he was of the same craft, he abode with them, and wrought: for by their occupation they were tentmakers.

19:11 – And God wrought special miracles by the hands of Paul:

19:12 – So that from his body were brought unto the sick handkerchiefs or aprons, and the diseases departed from them, and the evil spirits went out of them.

20:28 – Take heed therefore unto yourselves, and to all the flock, over the which the Holy Ghost hath made you overseers, to feed the church of God, which he hath purchased with his own blood.

28:6 – Howbeit they looked when he should have swollen, or fallen down dead suddenly: but after they had looked a great while, and saw no harm come to him, they changed their minds, and said that he was a god.

28:7 – In the same quarters were possessions of the chief man of the island, whose name was Publius; who received us, and lodged us three days courteously.

28:8 – And it came to pass, that the father of Publius lay sick of a fever and of a bloody flux: to whom Paul entered in, and prayed, and laid his hands on him, and healed him.

28:9 – So when this was done, others also, which had diseases in the island, came, and were healed:
28:27 – For the heart of this people is waxed gross, and their ears are dull of hearing, and their eyes have they closed; lest they should see with their eyes, and hear with their ears, and understand with their heart, and should be converted, and I should heal them.

Romans

4:25 – Who was delivered for our offences, and was raised again for our justification.
5:6 – For when we were yet without strength, in due time Christ died for the ungodly.
5:12 – Wherefore, as by one man sin entered into the world, and death by sin; and so death passed upon all men, for that all have sinned:
6:9 – Knowing that Christ being raised from the dead dieth no more; death hath no more dominion over him.
6:12 – Let not sin therefore reign in your mortal body, that ye should obey it in the lusts thereof.
6:13 – Neither yield ye your members as instruments of unrighteousness unto sin: but yield yourselves unto God, as those that are alive from the dead, and your members as instruments of righteousness unto God.
8:11 – But if the Spirit of him that raised up Jesus from the dead dwell in you, he that raised up Christ from the dead shall also quicken your mortal bodies by his Spirit that dwelleth in you.

8:13 – For if ye live after the flesh, ye shall die: but if ye through the Spirit do mortify the deeds of the body, ye shall live.

8:30 – Moreover whom he did predestinate, them he also called: and whom he called, them he also justified: and whom he justified, them he also glorified.

15:8 – Now I say that Jesus Christ was a minister of the circumcision for the truth of God, to confirm the promises made unto the fathers:

15:20 – Yea, so have I strived to preach the gospel, not where Christ was named, lest I should build upon another man's foundation:

15:21 – But as it is written, To whom he was not spoken of, they shall see: and they that have not heard shall understand.

1 Corinthians

4:11 – Even unto this present hour we both hunger, and thirst, and are naked, and are buffeted, and have no certain dwelling place;

4:12 – And labour, working with our own hands: being reviled, we bless; being persecuted, we suffer it:

5:7 – Purge out therefore the old leaven, that ye may be a new lump, as ye are unleavened. For even Christ our passover is sacrificed for us:

9:10 – Or saith he it altogether for our sakes? For our sakes, no doubt, this is written: that he that ploweth should plow in hope; and that he that thresheth in hope should be partaker of his hope.

10:23 – All things are lawful for me, but all things are not expedient: all things are lawful for me, but all things edify not.

11:27 – Wherefore whosoever shall eat this bread, and drink this cup of the Lord, unworthily, shall be guilty of the body and blood of the Lord.

11:28 – But let a man examine himself, and so let him eat of that bread, and drink of that cup.

11:29 – For he that eateth and drinketh unworthily, eateth and drinketh damnation to himself, not discerning the Lord's body.

11:30 – For this cause many are weak and sickly among you, and many sleep.

12:11 – But all these worketh that one and the selfsame Spirit, dividing to every man severally as he will.

12:28 – And God hath set some in the church, first apostles, secondarily prophets, thirdly teachers, after that miracles, then gifts of healings, helps, governments, diversities of tongues.

12:30 – Have all the gifts of healing? do all speak with tongues? do all interpret?

13:4 – For though he was crucified through weakness, yet he liveth by the power of God. For we also are weak in him, but we shall live with him by the power of God toward you.

13:8 – Charity never faileth: but whether there be prophecies, they shall fail; whether there be tongues, they shall cease; whether there be knowledge, it shall vanish away.

13:9 – For we know in part, and we prophesy in part.

13:10 – But when that which is perfect is come, then that which is in part shall be done away.
15:3 – For I delivered unto you first of all that which I also received, how that Christ died for our sins according to the scriptures;
15:37 – And that which thou sowest, thou sowest not that body that shall be, but bare grain, it may chance of wheat, or of some other grain:
16:20 – All the brethren greet you. Greet ye one another with an holy kiss.

2 Corinthians

4:11 – For we which live are alway delivered unto death for Jesus' sake, that the life also of Jesus might be made manifest in our mortal flesh.
5:21 – For he hath made him to be sin for us, who knew no sin; that we might be made the righteousness of God in him.
7:11 – For behold this selfsame thing, that ye sorrowed after a godly sort, what carefulness it wrought in you, yea, what clearing of yourselves, yea, what indignation, yea, what fear, yea, what vehement desire, yea, what zeal, yea, what revenge! In all things ye have approved yourselves to be clear in this matter.
12:10 – Therefore I take pleasure in infirmities, in reproaches, in necessities, in persecutions, in distresses for Christ's sake: for when I am weak, then am I strong.

Galatians

1:12 – For I neither received it of man, neither was I taught it, but by the revelation of Jesus Christ.

3:13 – Christ hath redeemed us from the curse of the law, being made a curse for us: for it is written, Cursed is every one that hangeth on a tree:

3:14 – That the blessing of Abraham might come on the Gentiles through Jesus Christ; that we might receive the promise of the Spirit through faith.

Ephesians

2:2 – Wherein in time past ye walked according to the course of this world, according to the prince of the power of the air, the spirit that now worketh in the children of disobedience:

2:3 – Among whom also we all had our conversation in times past in the lusts of our flesh, fulfilling the desires of the flesh and of the mind; and were by nature the children of wrath, even as others.

2:6 – And hath raised us up together, and made us sit together in heavenly places in Christ Jesus:

6:13 – Wherefore take unto you the whole armour of God, that ye may be able to withstand in the evil day, and having done all, to stand.

Philippians

2:6 – Who, being in the form of God, thought it not robbery to be equal with God:

2:7 – But made himself of no reputation, and took upon him the form of a servant, and was made in the likeness of men:
2:9 – Wherefore God also hath highly exalted him, and given him a name which is above every name:

Colossians

2:4 – And this I say, lest any man should beguile you with enticing words.
2:15 – And having spoiled principalities and powers, he made a shew of them openly, triumphing over them in it.

1 Timothy

3:16 – And without controversy great is the mystery of godliness: God was manifest in the flesh, justified in the Spirit, seen of angels, preached unto the Gentiles, believed on in the world, received up into glory.
4:5 – For it is sanctified by the word of God and prayer.
5:23 – Drink no longer water, but use a little wine for thy stomach's sake and thine often infirmities.

Hebrews

1:3 – Who being the brightness of his glory, and the express image of his person, and upholding all things by the word of his power, when he had by himself purged our sins, sat down on the right hand of the Majesty on high;

2:4 – God also bearing them witness, both with signs and wonders, and with divers miracles, and gifts of the Holy Ghost, according to his own will?

2:14 – Forasmuch then as the children are partakers of flesh and blood, he also himself likewise took part of the same; that through death he might destroy him that had the power of death, that is, the devil;

4:6 – Seeing therefore it remaineth that some must enter therein, and they to whom it was first preached entered not in because of unbelief:

5:5 – So also Christ glorified not himself to be made an high priest; but he that said unto him, Thou art my Son, today have I begotten thee.

8:6 – But now hath he obtained a more excellent ministry, by how much also he is the mediator of a better covenant, which was established upon better promises.

9:7 – But into the second went the high priest alone once every year, not without blood, which he offered for himself, and for the errors of the people:

9:12 – Neither by the blood of goats and calves, but by his own blood he entered in once into the holy place, having obtained eternal redemption for us.

9:19 – For when Moses had spoken every precept to all the people according to the law, he took the blood of calves and of goats, with water, and scarlet wool, and hyssop, and sprinkled both the book, and all the people,

9:12 – Neither by the blood of goats and calves, but by his own blood he entered in once into the holy place, having obtained eternal redemption for us.

9:22 – And almost all things are by the law purged with blood; and without shedding of blood is no remission.

9:24 – For Christ is not entered into the holy places made with hands, which are the figures of the true; but into heaven itself, now to appear in the presence of God for us:

9:26 – For then must he often have suffered since the foundation of the world: but now once in the end of the world hath he appeared to put away sin by the sacrifice of himself.

10:1 – For the law having a shadow of good things to come, and not the very image of the things, can never with those sacrifices which they offered year by year continually make the comers thereunto perfect.

10:12 – But this man, after he had offered one sacrifice for sins for ever, sat down on the right hand of God;

10:20 – By a new and living way, which he hath consecrated for us, through the veil, that is to say, his flesh;

12:13 – And make straight paths for your feet, lest that which is lame be turned out of the way; but let it rather be healed.

James

1:25 – But whoso looketh into the perfect law of liberty, and continueth therein, he being not a forgetful hearer, but a doer of the work, this man shall be blessed in his deed.

4:7 – Submit yourselves therefore to God. Resist the devil, and he will flee from you.

5:14 – Is any sick among you? let him call for the elders of the church; and let them pray over him, anointing him with oil in the name of the Lord:

5:15 – And the prayer of faith shall save the sick, and the Lord shall raise him up; and if he have committed sins, they shall be forgiven him.

5:16 – Confess your faults one to another, and pray one for another, that ye may be healed. The effectual fervent prayer of a righteous man availeth much.

1 Peter

1:23 – Being born again, not of corruptible seed, but of incorruptible, by the word of God, which liveth and abideth for ever.

2:24 – Who his own self bare our sins in his own body on the tree, that we, being dead to sins, should live unto righteousness: by whose stripes ye were healed.

5:8 – Be sober, be vigilant; because your adversary the devil, as a roaring lion, walketh about, seeking whom he may devour:

2 Peter

2:1 – But there were false prophets also among the people, even as there shall be false teachers among you, who privily shall bring in damnable heresies, even denying the Lord that bought them, and bring upon themselves swift destruction.

Titus

1:15 – Unto the pure all things are pure: but unto them that are defiled and unbelieving is nothing pure; but even their mind and conscience is defiled.

1 John

4:10 – Herein is love, not that we loved God, but that he loved us, and sent his Son to be the propitiation for our sins.

5:18 – We know that whosoever is born of God sinneth not; but he that is begotten of God keepeth himself, and that wicked one toucheth him not.

5:19 – And we know that we are of God, and the whole world lieth in wickedness.

Revelation

5:9 – And they sung a new song, saying, Thou art worthy to take the book, and to open the seals thereof: for thou wast slain, and hast redeemed us to God by thy blood out of every kindred, and tongue, and people, and nation;